Understanding the HighScope Approach

Understanding the HighScope Approach is a much needed source of information for those wishing to extend and consolidate their understanding of the HighScope approach. It will enable the reader to analyse the essential elements of the HighScope approach to early childhood and its relationship to quality early years practice.

Exploring all areas of the curriculum, including the learning environment, plan-do-review, adult–child interaction and assessment, this book:

- describes the key principles of the HighScope approach to early childhood with examples from HighScope settings;
- provides students and practitioners with the relevant information about a key pedagogical influence on high-quality early years practice in the United Kingdom;
- highlights the key ideas that practitioners should consider when reviewing and reflecting on their own practice;
- can be used as the basis for continuing professional development and action research.

Written to support the work of all those in the field of early years education and childcare, this is a vital text for students, early years and childcare practitioners, teachers, early years professionals, children's centre professionals, lecturers, advisory teachers, head teachers and setting managers.

Monica Wiltshire provides training and consultancy for early years practitioners in the United Kingdom and Sweden. Her previous positions include Head of a Children's Centre, Inspector for Children's Services and Consultant Trainer for HighScope UK.

Understanding the. . . Approach

Series Editors: Pat Brunton and Linda Thornton

This new series provides a much needed source of information for those wishing to extend and consolidate their understanding of international approaches to early years education and childcare. The books will enable the reader to analyse the essential elements of each approach and its relationship to quality early years practice.

Each book:

- Describes the key principles of the approach to early childhood relating theory to practice through case studies and practical examples;
- Provides students and practitioners with the relevant information about a key pedagogical influence on high-quality early years practice;
- Highlights the key ideas that practitioners should consider when reviewing and reflecting on their own practice;
- Can be used as the basis for continuing professional development and reflective practice.

Written to support the work of all those in the field of early years education and childcare, these will be invaluable texts for students, early years and childcare practitioners, teachers, early years professionals, children's centre professionals, lecturers, advisory teachers, head teachers and setting managers.

Understanding the HighScope Approach

Early Years Education in Practice

Monica Wiltshire

Routledge
Taylor & Francis Group

LONDON AND NEW YORK

First published 2012
by Routledge
2 Park Square, Milton Park, Abingdon, Oxon OX14 4RN

Simultaneously published in the USA and Canada
by Routledge
711 Third Avenue, New York, NY 10017

Routledge is an imprint of the Taylor & Francis Group, an informa business

British Library Cataloguing in Publication Data
A catalogue record for this book is available from the British Library

Library of Congress Cataloging in Publication Data
Wiltshire, Monica.
  Understanding the high scope approach: early years education in practice /
Monica Wiltshire.
     p. cm.
  Includes index.
  1. Early childhood education – United States. 2. Active learning – United
States. I. Title.
  LB1139.35.u6W55 2011
  372.210973 – dc22   2011015891

ISBN: 978–0–415–58357–2 (hbk)
ISBN: 978–0–415–58358–9 (pbk)
ISBN: 978–0–203–80194–9 (ebk)

Typeset in Palatino and Futura
by Keystroke, Station Road, Codsall, Wolverhampton

Printed and bound in Great Britain by the MPG Books Group

Dedication

This book is dedicated to the late Dr David P. Weikart, whose vision for children inspired me, as it has so many others across the world.

Contents

Illustrations

Figures

Table

Boxes

Introduction

A personal perspective

Many children, families and practitioners have been touched by High-Scope and describe the approach as inspirational. I first came across HighScope in 1989 whilst on my social work training. As the head of an inner London children's centre at that time, I was all too aware of the variations in practice within my own setting, let alone across the country, and found that HighScope gives a coherent, co-ordinated curriculum of best practice for staff teams to work with, using a common language and way of working. I especially liked the practical focus, with lots of ideas to take away and try out, and the emphasis on the *process* and *how* to support children's learning, which then leads naturally to what we want young children to learn. With a clear reason behind every element of the approach, I was inspired and began my HighScope journey to find out more. I attended a two-day introductory course run by Pam Lafferty at the Institute. This led to me attending the sixth Training of Trainers Course, and so through to training as a HighScope Staff Consultant myself in 2001.

Background to the UK interest in the HighScope approach

HighScope is one of the key pedagogical approaches to early childhood education that has strongly influenced early years principles and practice in the UK. Based on a central belief in active learning, it was 'cutting edge' in 1984 when the first HighScope pilot project took place in the UK. From early days in VOLCUF (Voluntary Organisation Liaison Committee for Under Fives) premises in Holloway Road, North London, HighScope UK opened in 1990 as the first international institute outside of the USA. The headquarters in Penge, South East London, with training rooms, stock rooms and offices became a base for high-quality training and the dissemination of HighScope publications. Funded primarily by the children's charity Barnardos for twenty years, and with Kathy Sylva, who led the Effective Provision of Preschool Education (EPPE) research, as patron, HighScope UK achieved a very high profile in the sphere of early years education, informing key organisations and government policy. In 2007 HighScope relocated to the North East of England, with a demonstration preschool at South Tyneside Early Excellence Centre.

The aim of this book

Understanding the HighScope Approach has been written to give people in the early years field access to an accurate, factual overview of HighScope and thereby present its strengths, correct myths and address criticisms. Taken on its own it will provide a valuable stimulus to examine beliefs about what is important for young children and whether practice matches beliefs, or as part of this series it will provide a source for discussion, analysis and comparison between the leading approaches in early childhood education.

HighScope is used in many different countries and provides a flexible framework, with principles that transfer across different ages, settings, sectors and abilities. Readers will realise that implementing HighScope does not require specific materials or altering your basic beliefs about what is good for children. However, it needs to be said that HighScope is a philosophy, a way of thinking, and not something you do on a Friday afternoon, or in one room in your setting. Neither is it a curriculum that you 'take off the shelf' and implement in three weeks; it takes practice, commitment and motivation. Reference to training available can be found on the following websites for those who want to fully embrace the HighScope approach:

- www.highscope.org
- www.high-scope.org.uk.

The structure of the book

Each chapter will focus on an aspect of the approach, although it will be evident that they are all interrelated and none can be considered in isolation.

Chapter 1 describes where, how and why HighScope began and gives a biography of Dr David Weikart, who founded the approach. It includes theoretical influences and the research-based evidence in support of the HighScope curriculum. Based on these and other studies, it identifies elements of high-quality early years programmes.

Chapter 2 highlights the key principles of HighScope as shown in the Wheel of Learning. It serves as a brief introduction to help the reader understand how HighScope works and its educational philosophy before going into greater detail in subsequent chapters.

Chapter 3 focuses on active learning as the central element which drives the whole of the curriculum. It covers the five essential ingredients of active learning – materials, manipulation, choice, child language and thought, adult scaffolding and its natural outcomes of personal motivation and 'key developmental indicators' – the HighScope curriculum content.

Chapter 4 looks at how we can make the best possible use of space for active learners both indoors and outdoors. It looks at the logical organisation of space into interest areas, the types of materials that are appealing to children and the use of storage to enable a find-use-return cycle. This chapter includes a sample material list for a HighScope classroom.

Chapter 5 looks at how we can make the best use of time and apply the ingredients of active learning throughout the day, with a balance between adult-and child-initiated activities. It introduces practical strategies like the daily routine chart and the message board used at greeting time, shows how HighScope's unique plan-do-review sequence enhances child-initiated play and how to share control at large and small group times.

Chapter 6 covers the essence of HighScope, which is adult–child interaction. It looks at styles and strategies that scaffold children's learning, including how to encourage without praising, and a problem-solving approach to conflict.

Chapter 7 applies many of the strategies from the previous chapters to how HighScope practitioners work in teams to assess their work with children and evaluate how well the curriculum itself is working. It looks at how practitioners take anecdotal observations as the starting-point for the daily planning process and for child assessment and describes how teams maintain and develop effective curriculum practices.

Finally, Chapter 8 concludes by looking at the work of HighScope in the UK and abroad, its impact for children, families and society and ideas for the future.

The structure of the chapters

At the beginning of each chapter there is a brief summary of the content, followed by a more detailed description of the aspect under consideration. References to key texts are included to encourage readers to extend their own research and understanding of the HighScope approach. Each chapter is summarised in a set of ten key points to clarify the reader's understanding of HighScope. Finally, there is a section in each chapter entitled 'Reflections on the HighScope approach'. It is offered as a starting-point, not a comprehensive list. It reflects many of the questions I have been asked by educators involved in planning professional development initiatives for themselves and their colleagues, and is primarily designed to be used as a group exercise to highlight issues you may wish to consider as a team when reflecting on your practice.

Terminology

When writing about an international approach there is frequently a range of terminology used. For this book I have chosen to use 'practitioner' to refer to the teacher, teaching assistant or any adult who works with children; 'setting' to refer to the classroom, children's centre or place where children meet; and refer to children aged between 3 and 5 years as 'preschoolers' and children aged 1 to 3 as 'under-threes'. For consistency, children have been referred to as 'he' or 'him'.

Acknowledgements

I am indebted to Mary Hohmann, David P. Weikart and Ann Epstein, who wrote *Educating Young Children: The Complete Guide to the HighScope Preschool Curriculum*, and Ann Epstein, who wrote *Essentials of Active Learning in Preschools: Getting to know the HighScope Curriculum*, from which some of the material in this book is taken.

My thanks go to staff and children at Leapfrog Neighbourhood Nursery in Portsmouth, England and ABC All About Children Preschool in Gothenburg, Sweden, where I wrote accounts of my visits and took photographs for this book.

Finally, my thanks to the editors who have helped me to shape this book: Annamarie Kino, commissioning editor, Routledge; Linda Thornton and Pat Brunton, series editors and Ann Epstein, Senior Director of Curriculum Development, HighScope Educational Research Foundation.

Related reading

Sylva, K., Melhuish, E. C., Sammons, P., Siraj-Blatchford, I. and Taggart, B. (2004) *The Effective Provision of Pre-school Education (EPPE) Project: Final Report.* Nottingham: SureStart/DfES

1 History and research

This chapter starts by explaining how HighScope got its name. It then tells the story of how HighScope grew, from the problems of 1960s segregated society in America to becoming an international approach. It describes the research-based evidence in support of the HighScope curriculum, its theoretical influences, underlying educational philosophy and the components of high-quality children's programmes derived from these studies. Finally, it explains why HighScope works and its impact 50 years on. The publications that have tracked its development are included in the related reading section at the end of the chapter.

How HighScope got its name

Originally called 'The Cognitively Oriented Curriculum', HighScope got its name from a summer camp for adolescents in 1963 in Michigan in the USA. 'High' to signify their aspiration level and 'scope' to signify the breadth of vision they hoped to reach. When David Weikart, the founder of HighScope, left his job as Director of Special Services in 1970 to focus on research and curriculum development, the name was adopted for the corporate name HighScope Educational Research Foundation. The work of the foundation has expanded and evolved to the present and now includes departments that carry out an active programme of *research* to evaluate HighScope programmes and other educational initiatives; *curriculum development*; and *professional development* training and conferences. HighScope also operates a *Demonstration Preschool* to showcase the curriculum in practice, and the *HighScope Press*, which publishes curriculum, training and assessment materials. Although HighScope's principal work is in early childhood education, it also offers validated *assessment tools* and related training in early elementary education and programmes for adolescents. An *International Registry* maintains a list of certified individuals and accredited settings that have participated in HighScope training and met the rigorous standards for curriculum knowledge and practitioner skills.

Origins and research

David Weikart

In 1962, clinical psychologist Dr David P. Weikart (1931–2003), Director of Special Services for the Ypsilanti Public Schools in Michigan, USA, initiated the Perry Preschool Project (which later became known as the HighScope Perry Preschool Study). He designed this project in response to the persistent failure of students from Ypsilanti's poorest neighbourhoods to graduate from high school.

After four years at Oberlin College, a two-year tour of duty with the US Marine Corps in Korea and Japan and three years of graduate studies at the University of Michigan in Ann Arbor, David Weikart was eager to enter the workforce and make a contribution to society. In his role as a school psychologist and director of special services he was new on the scene and the first person to hold this position under new state funding. He was alarmed by the trends he found in educational achievement and to be working in a context where most people felt that IQ was a genetic trait and that one could assign a youngster's IQ with fair accuracy simply by knowing the address of the family. Over the previous 10 years of standardised achievement testing (1948–57), no class in the Perry elementary school, a predominantly African American school, ever exceeded the 10th percentile on national norms for any tested subject. Yet in the elementary school on the other side of town, which primarily served the children of white, middle-class university professionals, no class ever scored less than the 90th percentile (Weikart, 2004).

Perry Preschool project

Although the HighScope approach is now used in settings serving the full range of preschool-aged children, it was originally developed to serve at-risk children from poor neighbourhoods in Ypsilanti. This area experienced racial segregation in 1960s America. There were overwhelming educational problems, including 50 per cent of children under 10 years old repeating a year, less than half the children graduating from high school, a high ratio of juvenile delinquency, and low test scores and academic standing.

In searching for a solution to these problems, David Weikart and his colleagues focused on preschool education for 3- and 4-year-olds because they knew from research emerging at the time that the potential for learning at this age was strong and wondered if there was something they could do before children started school that would better equip them. This decision also avoided the complexity of district-wide school reform because provision for this age group was non-statutory. To provide programme structure, the Special Services committee considered using the standard nursery school approach of the day, which focused on children's social and emotional development (Sears and Dowley, 1963), but subsequently decided that they must focus more squarely on children's intellectual development to support children's future academic growth. Because a systematic and documented approach to these cognitive components of preschool education did not exist at that time, the Special Services committee consulted several outside experts who were university professors in child development and special education. After reviewing the proposals, the basic advice from the experts was not to operate the programme. They felt that 3- and 4-year-olds, especially from disadvantaged backgrounds, would not cope with a cognitively oriented curriculum and that it might actually harm the children. Whilst initially this was disappointing advice, David Weikart and his colleagues realised that these experts had unknowingly given them a legitimate research question: *Does participation by disadvantaged children in an early education programme improve their intellectual and academic abilities?* Or, to put it simply, does preschool work? With this challenging question to be answered, the HighScope Perry Preschool Study was conceived as a tightly designed research project that would compare two groups of children randomly assigned to treatment (preschool) and control (no preschool) conditions.

Politically, the early 1960s was a period of optimism about 'breaking the cycle of poverty' and 'inoculating' children against failure. Despite this, it was a bold step to take when research was not part of the Special Services remit and there was no obvious funding for a year of the programme, let alone four decades. It was also 'of a time' because it would not be ethical now to withhold preschool experiences from a control group of children, but at that time there was a genuine lack of knowledge about the benefits of preschool education.

Background to the project

The Special Services committee set three criteria for the preschool curriculum they would select. First, it had to be based on a coherent theory of teaching and learning. Second, it had to support each child's capacity to develop individual talents and abilities through on-going opportunities for active learning. Third, researchers and teachers had to be able to work as partners so that theory and practice received equal consideration. The preschool programme that was the subject of the study served 3- and 4-year-olds from 1962 to 1967.

Theoretical influences

With these criteria firmly in mind, David Weikart, along with teachers, administrators and psychologists, turned to the writings of Jean Piaget. They were initially drawn to Piaget's child development research by a summary of his work presented in *Intelligence and Experience* by J. McVicker Hunt (1961). Clearly, Piaget's theory of development supported the curriculum team's philosophical orientation toward active learning. Through a series of seminars and discussions the team began the work of building a classroom programme for 3- and 4-year-olds around processes, goals and content areas derived from Piaget's research. Gradually, however, a major decision affecting project organisation and curriculum development was forced by staff differences. Several researchers who were Piagetian scholars began to outline weekly lesson plans for the teachers, including correct and incorrect ways to promote children's development of cognitive skills. While the teaching staff welcomed the suggestions, they felt that they had a better understanding of the children and what experiences fitted best within the daily routine and adult–child relationships. They also felt these instructions were pushing them towards a curriculum that was more directive than they had originally envisioned and wanted to include some traditional nursery school practices that would also support children's social and emotional development.

At this point David Weikart formalised his position: the HighScope approach would draw upon child development theory such as Piaget's, but the application of theory had to be tempered by advice from experienced classroom teachers. Theirs would never be a classic, strictly

Piagetian-based approach and sought the related developmental theories of others like John Dewey (1938/1963) and Erik Erikson (1950) which supported the idea of active learning, initiative, child choices and decisions. Psychologist Sara Smilansky was a consultant to HighScope in the early 1960s and urged curriculum developers to add the concept of recall to planning and work time so that children could reflect on their plans and actions and thereby gain more understanding of what they had learned in the process. The work of developmental psychologist and educator Lev Vygotsky (1934/1962) informed HighScope's interaction strategies to scaffold children's learning. As the approach has evolved, work on interaction styles has been informed by Virginia Satir (1994), and the work of Howard Gardener (1993) on multiple intelligences, amongst others, has informed the development of the 'key developmental indicators' – the 'curriculum content' that specifies the knowledge and skills that are appropriate for young children to learn.

The educational philosophy underlying HighScope is constructivist, as opposed to behaviourist (Watson 1928, Skinner 1983), and is best described by Alfie Kohn (1993 p. 219), who has informed much of HighScope's work on encouragement versus praise:

> People learn by actively constructing knowledge, weighing new information against their previous understanding, thinking about and working through discrepancies (on their own and with others), and coming to a new understanding. In a classroom faithful to constructivist views, students are afforded numerous opportunities to explore phenomena or ideas, conjecture, share hypotheses with others, and revise their original thinking. Such a classroom differs sharply from one in which the teacher lectures exclusively, explains the 'right way' to solve a problem without asking students to make some sense of their own, or denies the importance of students' own experiences or prior knowledge.

With these child development theoretical influences in mind, the HighScope curriculum came into being. David Weikart, in his book *How HighScope Grew: A Memoir* (2004 p. 67) states:

> Thus today, the HighScope curriculum is an amalgam of related developmental theories hammered into usefulness by decades of teacher experiences in the classroom and on home visits. I have never regretted this decision nor questioned the results. When I see our approach being used throughout the United States and in over 20 countries by a wide range of ethnic, religious and language groups, I see its broad accessibility as support for my decision to listen carefully to the teachers.

The people and organisations involved

All the study participants were African American, as was almost every-one in the Perry School neighbourhood where the research took place. The 123 children in the sample were randomly assigned by the flip of a coin to the 'programme group' or 'no programme group'. This decision was key because the only difference between the members of the two groups that can be traced back is their preschool experience, and this offers the best explanation for the findings of the research. The two groups were matched on mean socioeconomic status, mean intellectual performance and percentages of boys and girls. Five waves of children entered the project run at the Perry School between 1962 and 1967.

How the research was carried out

Four teachers with bachelor's degrees held daily classes of 20–25 chil-dren aged 3 to 4 years and made two home visits a week to share curriculum principles with parents; the adult–child ratios were arranged to allow for individualised as well as group scaffolding of learning and also to accommodate this high level of family involvement. With con-sistent curriculum training, supervision and assessment, the researchers and preschool teachers developed a comprehensive preschool approach. Based on the writings of theorists Piaget, Dewey and Smilansky, they educated children by having them *plan, do* and *review* their own learning activities, with the concept of active participatory learning central to every element of the curriculum. Researchers then assessed the status of the two groups annually from ages 3 to 11, at age 14–15, at age 19, 27 and 40 using variables representing certain characteristics, abilities, attitudes and type of performance. Retention of the study participants has been remarkable, largely due to the persistence and tenacity of the inter-viewers, and HighScope plans to interview the study groups again at ages 60–65.

The findings

All the findings of the Perry Preschool Project are reported in a series of monographs noted in the related reading section at the end of this chapter; the most recent findings being reported in *Life Time Effects* (Schweinhart et al. 2005). Researchers found that although there were some encouraging findings during and after the subjects' school years, the really interesting data began to emerge at age 27. The Age 27 findings showed that, in comparison with the 'no programme' group, the 'programme group' had:

- significantly higher monthly earnings at age 27 (with 29% vs 7% earning $2,000 or more per month
- significantly higher percentages of home ownership (36% vs 13%) and second car ownership (30% vs 13%)
- a significantly higher percentage of schooling completed (with 71% vs 54% completing 12th grade or higher)
- a significantly lower percentage receiving social services at some time in the previous 10 years (59% vs 80%)
- significantly fewer arrests by age 27 (with 7% vs 35% having five or more arrests), including significantly fewer arrests for crimes of drug taking or dealing (7% vs 25%).

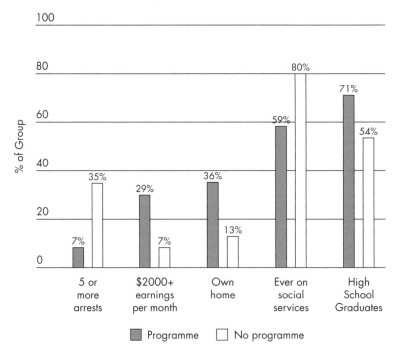

**HighScope Perry Preschool Study:
Major Findings at Age 27**

Figure 1.1 HighScope Preschool Study major findings at age 27

Source: Hohmann and Weikart (2002, p. 8)

The most compelling finding was the reduction in criminality, indicating social responsibility as a major outcome of the project. The Age 40 findings remain consistent, but with less difference in criminality, presumably because people commit less crime as they get older. The strengths of the crime-related findings underline the importance of social and emotional development in early years; this is a non-cognitive effect but related to impulse control, a need for attention and emotional intelligence in general.

Of specific interest to the policy makers are the cost savings to society, with fewer resources needed for special programmes, welfare benefits and, most significantly, savings in crime costs. The Age 40 study reports a return of $17 per dollar invested. David Weikart's economic analysis was new to the field, and evidence that high-quality early childhood education is a good public investment. This attention to the economic benefits to society of investing in early childhood education helped to garner widespread, bipartisan support for such initiatives.

What was it in the preschool curriculum that caused the results?

The studies revealed that it was not only academic content that was the link between an early childhood programme and successful adult

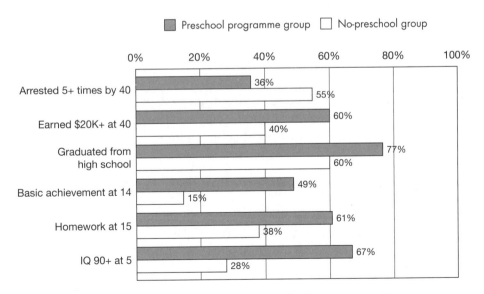

Figure 1.2 HighScope Preschool Study major findings at age 40

Source: Hohmann, Weikart and Epstein (2008, p. 8)

performance, but the development of specific personal and social dispositions. Erikson (1963) pointed out that the typical psychological thrust of a 3- to 5-year-old is towards developing a sense of initiative, responsibility and independence. Katz and Chard (1993), discussing the importance of children developing the dispositions of curiosity, friendliness and co-operation, pointed out that good preschool programmes support the development of such traits. However, personal dispositions are elusive and cannot be taught directly. Instead, they can only gradually emerge, under the right circumstances, as the by-products of children's engagement in developmentally appropriate, active learning experiences. It is HighScope's unique plan-do-review process that is strongly represented in the Perry Study. These three aspects of an active learning approach – children's expression of intent, their independently generated experiences and their reflections – define child-initiated learning. The outcomes are vital to life-long learning and include the development of such important dispositions as initiative, responsibility, curiosity, trust, confidence, independence and divergent thinking. These traits, valued by society, are the foundations of effective, socially responsible adulthood. When children participate in an active learning approach, they develop self-control and self-discipline. This control is real power, not over other people or things, but over themselves. Understanding what is happening in the surrounding environment, realising that those around them are genuinely interested in what they say and do, and knowing that their efforts have a chance of leading to success can give a sense of control that promotes personal satisfaction and motivates children to be productive. This creates a 'causal path' where the positive results transmit from one stage to the next, through to adulthood. While no single factor assures success in life, the sense of personal control is certainly a major force. A high-quality, active learning preschool programme supports and strengthens this disposition.

Conclusions drawn from the Perry Preschool Project

At Age 40 the study concluded that any preschool or childcare programme can have long-term effects benefitting social responsibility, earning and economic status, educational performance and family stability if its teachers:

- help children participate in their own education by having them plan, do and review their own activities

- receive consistent curriculum training, supervision and assessment
- have bachelor's degrees and certification in education
- hold daily classes for 3- and 4-year-olds, including those at risk of school failure
- have a strong and genuine partnership with parents.

Scientifically, the renowned HighScope Perry Preschool research is a major resource because of its excellent design and execution. It is a prospective, controlled-trials, longitudinal study of substantial duration, with astonishingly little attrition. The researchers have chosen to assess real-life outcomes of considerable importance. Instead of relying solely on self-reports, they have conducted an impressive search of educational, criminal and social service records that validates and gives great weight to their findings. Therefore the results of this study need to be taken very seriously. They show that it is possible to use early intervention to change the life prospects of children living in poverty, and that it is cost-effective to do so.

Other important research

In addition to the HighScope Perry Preschool Study described above, evidence for the effectiveness of HighScope's preschool curriculum comes from two other studies.

The HighScope Preschool Curriculum Comparison Study

This study, reported in *Lasting Differences* (Schweinhart and Weikart, 1997), also examines the long-term effects of preschool on children from low-income families. It compares 68 preschoolers randomly assigned to one of three different curriculum models: HighScope (Hohmann and Weikart, 2002), a traditional nursery school curriculum (Sears & Dowley, 1963) and a direct instruction model (Bereiter and Engelmann, 1966). The data, analysed through age 23, finds no significant and lasting group differences on language, literacy or school achievement. However, adults who attended the direct instruction programme as children have had consistently higher rates of criminal activity, as compared to the other two groups.

The HighScope National Training of Trainers Evaluation

This study, reported in *Training for Quality* (Epstein, 1993), surveyed 203 HighScope trainers, interviewed and observed 366 teachers in High-Scope and non-HighScope early childhood settings and assessed 200 preschool children in HighScope and comparison classrooms. It found positive results at all levels, for supervisors, teachers and children. The findings especially showcased the importance of the plan-do-review sequence in children's learning. The more teachers provided opportunities for children to plan and review activities of their own choice, the higher the children scored on measures of the academic and social skills needed for school success.

Independent studies likewise confirm that preschool children attending well-run HighScope programmes do better than those in other programme settings. Studies in the UK (Sylva, 1992) and the Netherlands (Veen, Roeleveld and Leseman, 2000) again found that when children plan, carry out and review their own learning activities, they play with more purpose and perform better on measures of language and intellectual development.

The outcomes of the research

Derived from research studies, HighScope identified seven basic elements of high-quality early years programmes:

- a child-development curriculum with active participatory learning
- good adult–child ratios so that adults can give individualised attention to children
- staff trained in early childhood development so that they can observe, understand and support children's learning in all areas
- supervisory support and in-service training so that staff can understand and carry out the curriculum
- involvement of parents as partners because they are children's first and most lasting teachers
- sensitivity to the non-educational needs of children and their families because preschool is just one component of children's early experiences

- developmentally appropriate evaluation procedures to accurately measure what children know and to plan effective ways to extend their learning.

Adapted from *A School Administrator's Guide to Early Childhood Programmes* (Schweinhart, 2004 p. 15)

Why HighScope works, and its impact today

In *Educating Young Children*, Hohmann, Weikart and Epstein (2008) say the HighScope approach is successful because:

Since its beginnings, the HighScope preschool approach has encouraged children to develop initiative by participating as active learners within a supportive social context. During the daily plan-do-review process children express, carry out and then reflect on their intentions. Throughout the day, children develop their own interests, generate ways to answer their own questions, and discuss their ideas with others. Supported by adults who are genuinely interested in what they say and do, children are able to construct their own understanding of the world around them and gain a sense of control and personal satisfaction. The HighScope curriculum works because its unflagging attention to children's strengths and abilities empowers children to follow through on their interests purposefully and creatively. In the process, children develop trust, initiative, curiosity, resourcefulness, independence, and responsibility – habits of mind that will serve them well throughout their lives.

(p. 10)

Although, compared to today's research programmes into the benefits of early childhood education, the Perry Preschool Project was a small sample (123 participants), it continues to be widely recognised and referred to by educational psychologists, criminologists and economists. David Weikart has taken his place amongst the pioneers of early education, developed an internationally respected approach and provided solid information from both the research findings and curriculum practices upon which to build in the future.

Key points

1. HighScope originated in 1960s America and is now an international approach.
2. HighScope is the only approach to early childhood education that has been validated by extensive, controlled, longitudinal research.
3. HighScope is most widely known for the Perry Preschool research, which started in 1962 to address concerns that many children were being failed by the school system. This led to the hypothesis that early intervention could prevent later problems.
4. The most compelling finding of the HighScope Perry Preschool research was the reduction in criminality, indicating social responsibility as a major outcome.
5. The economic analysis of the HighScope Perry Preschool research reported a return of $17 for every $1 spent.
6. The HighScope approach grew out of a need for a high-quality curriculum for the programme participants and was devised by researchers and teachers together. This researcher–practitioner partnership was unique to HighScope at that time, and continues to this day.
7. The HighScope approach pulls together the work of many theorists, practitioners and researchers to create a curriculum of best practice.
8. The educational philosophy underlying HighScope is constructivist.
9. Whilst the HighScope approach has evolved over time, the core principle of active participatory learning devised in 1962 remains the same today.
10. HighScope works because, as active learners within a supportive classroom community, children develop a sense of initiative and pro-social dispositions that positively affect their subsequent learning and life decisions.

Reflections on the HighScope approach

1. Origins and influences
   - Can you 'tell the story' of your setting?
   - Which theorists have influenced your practice and beliefs, and why?
   - Which practitioners have influenced your practice and beliefs, and why?

2. A common curriculum
   - What common values and beliefs are shared across your setting?
   - What practices demonstrate this, allowing for developmentally appropriate practice?
   - How would it feel for a child making the transition from a toddler room to a preschool room?
   - How would it feel to be a peripatetic staff member in your setting?
3. Dispositions for learning
   - What dispositions do you want for children?
   - Is this reflected in your mission statement or brochure?
   - Does your practice match your beliefs?
4. Defining quality
   - How does your setting meet the key elements of quality identified by HighScope researchers?
   - Which would you like to develop?
   - Do you have any to add?
5. Reflective practitioners
   - Which of your practices have remained constant throughout your career?
   - What practices have you added?
   - What practices have you discarded?

References

Bereiter, C., & Engelmann, S. (1966) *Teaching the Disadvantaged Child in the Preschool*. Englewood Cliffs, NJ: Prentice-Hall

Dewey, J. (1938/1963) *Experience and Education*. New York: Macmillan

Epstein, A. S. (1993) *Training for Quality: Improving Early Childhood Programmes through Systematic Inservice Training*. Ypsilanti, MI: HighScope Press

Erikson, E. (1950) *Childhood and Society*. New York: Norton

Erikson, E. (1963) *Childhood and Society* (2nd edn). New York: W. W. Norton

Gardener, H. (1993) *Frames of Mind. The Theory of Multiple Intelligences*. Great Britain: Fontana Press

Hohmann, M., Weikart, D. P. & Epstein, A. S. (2008) *Educating Young Children: Active Learning Practices for Preschool and Child Care Programmes* (3rd edn). Ypsilanti, MI: HighScope Press

Hunt, J. M. (1961) *Intelligence and Experience*. New York: Ronald Press

Katz, L. G., & Chard, S. C. (1993) The Project Approach. In J. L. Roopnarine & J. E. Johnson (eds), *Approaches to Early Childhood Education* (2nd edn, pp. 209–22). New York: Macmillan

Kohn, A. (1993) *Punished by Rewards: the Trouble with Gold Stars, Incentive Plans, A's, Praise and Other Bribes.* Boston: Houghton, Mifflin

Satir, V. (1994) *Peoplemaking.* USA: Souvenir Press

Schweinhart, L. J. (2004) *A School Administrator's Guide to Early Childhood Programmes* (2nd edn). Ypsilanti, MI: HighScope Press

Schweinhart, L. J., & Weikart, D. P. (1997) *Lasting Differences: The HighScope Preschool Curriculum Comparison Study through Age 23.* Ypsilanti, MI: HighScope Press

Schweinhart, L. J. et al. (2005) *Life Time Effects: The HighScope Perry Preschool Study through Age 40.* Ypsilanti, MI: HighScope Press

Sears, P. S., & Dowley, E. M. (1963) Research on Teaching in the Nursery School. In N. L. Gage (ed.), *Handbook of Research on Teaching.* Chicago: Rand McNally

Skinner, B. F. (1983) *A Matter of Consequences.* New York: Knopf.

Sylva, K. (1992) Conversations in the Nursery: How they Contribute to Aspirations and Plans, *Language and Education*, 6(2), 141–48

Veen, A., Roeleveld, J., & Leseman, P. (2000 January) *Evaluatie van Kaleidoscoop en Piramide Eindrapportage.* Sco Kohnstaff Instituut, Universiteit van Amsterdam

Vygotsky, L. S. (1934/1962) *Thought and Language.* Cambridge, MA: MIT Press

Watson, J. B. (1928) *Psychological Care of Infant and Child.* New York: Norton

Weikart, D. P. (2004) *How HighScope Grew: A Memoir.* Ypsilanti, MI: HighScope Press

Related reading

Mooney, C. (2000) *Theories of Childhood. An Introduction to Dewey, Montessori, Erikson, Piaget and Vygotsky.* Redleaf Press

Publications that track the development of the HighScope approach

1971	*The Cognitively Oriented Curriculum: A Framework for Preschool Educators*, by David Weikart, Linda Rogers, Carolyn Adcock, & Donna McClelland
1979	*Young Children in Action: A Manual for Preschool Educators*, by Mary Hohmann, Bernard Banet, & David Weikart
1986–present	HighScope Extensions: Newsletters of the HighScope Curriculum
1989–present	The Teacher's Idea Book Series by HighScope Staff and field consultants
1991–2005	*Supporting Young Learners: Ideas for Preschool and Day Care Providers*, Volumes 1–4 by HighScope Staff and field consultants
1995, 2002 & 2008	*Educating Young Children: Active Learning Practices for Preschool and Child Care Programmes*, by Mary Hohmann, David Weikart, & Ann Epstein

2002   *You Can't Come to My Birthday Party: Conflict Resolution with Young Children*, by Betsy Evans

2003a   *Preschool Child Observation Record (COR)*, 2nd edn

2003   *Preschool Programme Quality Assessment (PQA)*, 2nd edn

2005   *Growing Readers Early Literacy Curriculum*, by Andrea DeBruin-Parecki, & Mary Hohmann

2007   *Essentials of Active Learning in Preschool: Getting to Know the HighScope Curriculum*, by Ann Epstein

Monographs of the HighScope Educational Research Foundation

No. 1 *Longitudinal Results of the Ypsilanti Preschool Project*, by D. P. Weikart, D. J. Deloria, S. A. Lawser, & R. Wiegerink (1970) Reprint 1993

No. 2 *Home Teaching with Mothers and Infants: The Ypsilanti-Carnegie Infant Education Project – An Experiment*, by D. Z. Lambie, J. T. Bond, & D. P. Weikart 1974

No. 3 *The Ypsilanti Perry Preschool Project: Preschool Years and Longitudinal Results through Fourth Grade*, by D. P. Weikart, J. T. Bond, & J. T. McNeil 1978

No. 4 *The Ypsilanti Preschool Curriculum Demonstration Project: Preschool Years and Longitudinal Results*, by D. P. Weikart, A. S. Epstein, L. J. Schweinhart, & J. T. Bond 1978

No. 5 *An Economic Analysis of the Ypsilanti Perry Preschool Project*, by C. U. Beber, P. W. Foster, & D. P. Weikart 1978

No. 6 *The Ypsilanti-Carnegie Infant Education Project: Longitudinal Follow-Up*, by A. S. Epstein & D. P. Weikart 1979

No. 7 *Young Children Grow Up: The Effects of the Perry Preschool Program on Youths through Age 15*, by L. J. Schweinhart & D. P. Weikart 1980

No. 8 *Changed Lives: The Effects of the Perry Preschool Program on Youths through Age 19*, by J. R. Berrueta-Clement, L. J. Schweinhart, W. S. Barnett, A. S. Epstein, & D. P. Weikart 1984

No. 9 *Training for Quality: Improving Early Childhood Programs through Systematic Inservice Training*, by A. S. Epstein 1993

No. 10 *Significant Benefits: The HighScope Perry Preschool Study through Age 27*, by L. J. Schweinhart, H. V. Barnes, & D. P. Weikart, with W. S. Barnett, & A. S. Epstein 1993

No. 11 *Lives in the Balance: Age 27 Benefit-Cost Analysis of the HighScope Perry Preschool Program*, by W. S. Barnett 1996

No. 12 *Lasting Differences: The HighScope Preschool Curriculum Comparison Study through Age 23*, by L. J. Schweinhart, & D. P. Weikart 1997

No. 13 *Supporting Families with Young Children: The HighScope Parent-To-Parent Dissemination Project* by A. S. Epstein, J. Montie, & D. P. Weikart 2002

No. 14 *Life Time Effects: The HighScope Perry Preschool Study through Age 40*, by L. J. Schweinhart, J. Montie, Z. Xiang, W. S. Barnett, C. R. Belfield, & M. Nores 2005

2 An overview of HighScope

This chapter highlights the key principles of HighScope and how they are shown graphically in the HighScope Preschool Wheel of Learning. It outlines the five aspects of the HighScope approach illustrated in the Wheel of Learning diagrams and shows how they relate to one another. The five aspects of the HighScope approach are each explained in more detail in the subsequent chapters of this book.

The HighScope approach for preschool children

The key principles of the HighScope approach are that children learn best when:

- they have active involvement with people, materials and ideas
- they plan and carry out activities of their own choosing and reflect on them
- their work is supported by adults who share control with children.

The HighScope Preschool Wheel of Learning graphically represents the practical elements of the key principles of the HighScope approach and how they fit together. In the centre of the wheel 'active learning' underpins the four equally important areas of practice and responsibility:

- the learning environment
- the daily routine
- adult–child interaction
- assessment.

Figure 2.1 The HighScope Wheel of Learning

Source: Hohmann, Weikart and Epstein (2008, p. 6)

Each area is interrelated and interconnected. For example, the practicalities of adult–child interaction – interaction strategies, encouragement and a problem-solving approach to conflict – apply to each segment of the daily routine: plan-do-review, small group time and large group time.

The Wheel of Learning is a framework of guidelines for establishing and operating high-quality active learning settings for young children which has been in place since the inception of HighScope. The structure of this book is based on the Wheel of Learning, to enable the reader to understand the HighScope approach and compare and contrast it with other early years approaches.

Active learning

Active learning refers to how young children construct their knowledge of the world. It means that children participate actively in the learning process and gain knowledge through direct experiences with people, objects, events and ideas. Although they will be supported by adults and peers in a HighScope setting, the children have to do things for themselves. Every aspect of HighScope is designed to allow active learning to happen, so as to ensure this key principle relates to everyday practice. When the process of active learning is in place the outcomes of the approach are both the disposition of initiative and the content of the curriculum, which are known as the 'key developmental indicators' in the HighScope approach.

Initiative

The power of active learning comes from personal initiative, wanting to do something for yourself rather than to please someone else. Central to the HighScope approach is a belief that young children have an innate desire to explore and discover. They ask and search for answers to questions, they solve problems that stand in the way of their goals and they generate new strategies to try. They want to do things for themselves. The HighScope approach recognises and supports this by encouraging children to use their initiative, to plan and to develop their own strengths and interests.

Key developmental indicators (KDIs)

The key developmental indicators are the experiences children engage in during the course of their play that reflect their developing mental, emotional, social and physical abilities. HighScope has defined the KDIs in a series of 58 statements which describe the curriculum content (see Box 3.2).[1]

As children play – for example, as they fit things together, take them apart, make things or pretend – they learn and gain a sense of competence. For HighScope practitoners the KDIs give meaning to what children are

---

1 HighScope is currently updating the KDIs based on the latest research in child development and effective teaching practices. For updates to the KDIs, visit the website: http://www.highscope.org/Content.asp?ContentId=566.

doing. Practitioners use the KDIs as tools for observing, describing and supporting children's development.

Active learning is discussed in more detail in Chapter 3.

The learning environment

The HighScope approach places a strong emphasis on planning the layout of the setting and the nature of the materials available to children. An active learning environment needs to provide children with on-going opportunities to be independent, to make choices and decisions and to use their initiative.

Areas

HighScope practitioners organise the play space into specific interest areas to support the types of play young children enjoy – sand and water, building, pretending, drawing and painting, creating things, using books and playing simple games. These interest areas are defined by low physical boundaries and are called by simple names that make sense to the children, for example, the house area, the sand and water area.

Materials

The interest areas contain a wide and plentiful assortment of easily accessible materials which children can choose and use to carry out their intentions and ideas for play. There is a balance of natural, found, commercial and home-made materials which will provide many opportunities each day for children to engage with curriculum content in creative and purposeful ways.

Storage

HighScope practitioners arrange storage for materials using low shelves, storage containers and baskets with picture labels the children can read, so all children can independently find, use and return the items they need.

The learning environment is developed in more detail in Chapter 4.

Daily routine

HighScope practitioners plan a consistent yet flexible daily routine – consistent so that children feel secure in knowing what will happen next and flexible so that practitioners can use their judgement about spontaneous opportunities that may arise. The day will have a balance between child- and adult-initiated activities.

Plan-do-review

Time for plan-do-review – also called planning time, work time and recall time – is the child-initiated period of the day.

Planning is a process in which children learn to create and express intentions. In a group or individually, and supported by an adult, children plan what they wish to do. Children's planning becomes increasingly sophisticated as they become conversant with the process. At work time children generate experiences – things to do – based upon their plans. Children need time for trial and error, to generate new ideas, practise and succeed, and practitioners will actively observe and participate in children's play. This commonly includes pretending and role playing, building block structures, reading books and drawing. Work time is followed by tidy-up time, during which children return the materials they used to their storage places. Then, during review time children reflect on their experiences, with increasing verbal ability and logic as they mature.

Small group time

Small group time is initiated by the practitioners. They select new or familiar materials based on their observations of children's interests, the KDIs and local traditions or seasonal activities that are part of the children's lives. Small group time is a distinct time during the day when the same group of children and adults work together.

Large group time

During large group time children experience active learning collectively – all children and all adults engaged in enjoyable shared experiences. Practitioners plan the large group time session in advance. It may include music and movement activities, story-telling, group discussions and cooperative play and projects within which children will have opportunities to initiate ideas.

In addition, HighScope settings have other group times that include sensitively handling greetings and departures, looking at the message board, sharing a snack or a meal in a relaxed social setting and playing outside. HighScope also offers practical suggestions for dealing with the transitions between these parts of the daily routine.

Chapter 5 looks at daily routines in more detail.

Adult–child interaction

HighScope practitioners believe that it is important to provide a psychologically safe climate for young learners and they strive to be supportive as they converse and play with children.

Interaction strategies

There are several interaction strategies that HighScope practitioners commonly use. These include sharing control with children, focusing on children's strengths, forming authentic relationships with children, supporting children's play, using encouragement instead of praise and adopting a problem-solving approach to social conflict. These strategies are intended to enable the child to express thoughts and feelings freely and confidently, to decide on the direction and content of conversations and to experience true partnership in dialogue.

Encouragement

HighScope practitioners motivate children by taking time to notice their contributions and efforts and by describing their work. For example, 'You spent a long time on your painting and used blue and red paint.' This supports children's intrinsic motivation to learn and demonstrates sharing control between adults and children.

Problem-solving approach to conflict

HighScope practitioners use a problem-solving approach to conflict rather than a child-management system based on praise, punishment and reward. They view conflicts as opportunities to support the learning of social and emotional skills through using positive interaction strategies which stop hurtful actions and address children's feelings, thoughts and needs. This relationship with children is seen as having long-term as well as immediate benefits because it demonstrates to children how to form positive relationships for themselves.

Chapter 6 looks in more detail at adult–child interaction.

Assessment

Assessment in HighScope is twofold and includes assessment both of children's learning and development and of the effectiveness of the curriculum. It encompasses all the tasks carried out by the team, including recording observations, daily team planning, a summative developmental record for each child and assessment of every aspect of the received curriculum. Assessment is used to evaluate whether or not the aims of the curriculum are in place – that active learning is happening, that there are opportunities to problem-solve, be independent, make decisions and use initiative and that there is a balance between care and education.

Teamwork

Teamwork is the starting-point for assessment because it includes an evaluation of everything the team does. To help practitioners work well together in the HighScope approach teamwork is built on supportive adult relationships where there is open communication, individual differences are respected and there is patience with the teamwork process. Practitioner teams and supervisor–practitioner teams use a variety of observation based assessment strategies – the Programme Implementation Profile (PIP) and Observation/Feedback – to plan for individual children and the group as a whole, assess the fidelity of curriculum implementation and develop a plan for on-going in-service staff training to improve teaching practices.

Daily anecdotal notes

A unifying task supporting HighScope teamwork is making daily anecdotal observations of children. These observations are brief descriptions of something a child has done or said that is significant to his development. They are recorded under the curriculum content (KDIs) headings.

Daily planning

Before children arrive, after the children leave or while the children are resting, practitioners engage in a daily planning session in which they share their observations of children, analyse the observations in terms of the KDIs and make plans for the next day.

Child assessment

Formative assessment is the type of assessment based on on-going observations, photographs and samples of work. Summative assessment is a summary of all the formative assessments, made once or twice a year, and makes statements about a child's achievements. Periodically, the team will condense the child observations they have noted to complete a summative assessment for each child using the *Preschool Child Observation Record (COR)* (2003a).

Assessment of children and curriculum implementation is discussed in more detail in Chapter 7.

The HighScope approach for under-threes

HighScope is a flexible framework which is transferable across different ages, abilities and sectors. In the HighScope Infant and Toddler Wheel of Learning the same five principles for preschool children also apply to children under three.

The main differences between the two are in the section 'schedules and routines', where emphasis is placed on 'arrivals and departures' and 'caregiving routines: eating, sleeping and bodily care'. Choice time is child initiated and is the developmental precursor to plan-do-review. Similarly, group time is adult initiated and more fluid and dynamic than preschool small group time and large group time, to match the developmental needs of this younger age group.

Partnership with parents

The HighScope approach recognises parents as children's first and foremost educators. Working in partnership with parents is believed to

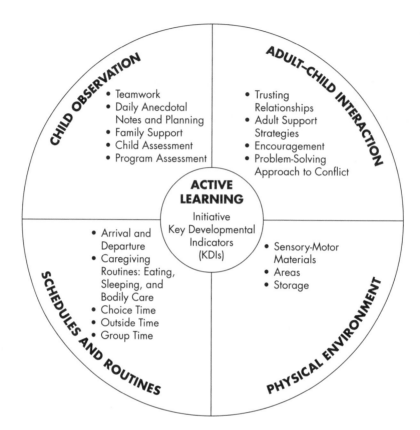

Figure 2.2 The HighScope Infant and Toddler Wheel of Learning

Source: Post, Hohmann and Epstein (2011, p. 3)

be very important and means that information is shared in both direc-
tions. Parents educate practitioners about their children and practitioners
offer insights into child development and how the curriculum supports
learning. Parents' understanding of the curriculum leads to greater consistency for the child and bridges the gap between home and setting.

The principles and practices of active learning shown in the wheel of
learning apply equally to guide practitioners' work with parents and
carers in both the home and daily interactions; for example, focusing on
family strengths and a problem-solving approach to conflict resolution.
The relationship is characterised by mutual respect.

Key points

1. HighScope is an educational philosophy which recognises the uniqueness of each child and develops their self-confidence by building on what children *can* do and using that as the starting-point for teaching.
2. The HighScope Preschool Wheel of Learning illustrates how the approach works. It shows the five aspects which form the framework of the HighScope approach, active learning, the learning environment, daily routine, adult–child interaction and assessment.
3. Active learning is the central and most important part which guides practitioners' beliefs about how children learn.
4. Children have an inborn desire to be active learners; HighScope practitioners work with and extend this natural instinct, so learning opportunities multiply.
5. The key developmental indicators are readily apparent in children's active learning and form the content of the curriculum.
6. The learning environment describes how thought is given to the organisation of space for active learners.
7. The daily routine describes how practitioners make the most effective use of time for active learners, with a balance between adult- and child-initiated activities.
8. Active learning depends on positive adult–child interactions.
9. Assessment in the HighScope approach means working in teams to support and build on children's interests and strengths, guided by the curriculum and using curriculum assessment to monitor fidelity to the approach and plan practitioner training.
10. The HighScope approach remains true to its original vision of half a century ago.

Reflections on the HighScope approach

1. Wheel of Learning
   ■ How would you arrange your key principles in a blank wheel of learning?
   ■ What would go in the centre circle?
2. Tell it in an hour!
   ■ How would you go about giving a short introductory talk on your work?

- Which elements of your practice would you include?
3. A cohesive curriculum
   - How does your learning environment impact on your daily routine?
   - What other links and connections can you see between the different aspects of your practice?
4. Understanding HighScope
   - What aspects of your practice can you see in the HighScope approach?
   - What sets HighScope apart from your practice?
   - What would you like to know more about?
5. Educational philosophy
   - What are your beliefs about teaching and learning?
   - How do your beliefs affect your teaching, assessment and planning?
   - Does your practice match your beliefs?

References

Hohmann, M., Weikart, D. P. & Epstein, A. S. (2008) *Educating Young Children: Active Learning Practices for Preschool and Child Care Programmes* (3rd edn). Ypsilanti, MI: HighScope Press

Post, J., Hohmann, M., & Epstein, A. S. (2011) *Tender Care and Early Learning: Supporting Infants and Toddlers in Child Care Settings* (2nd edn). Ypsilanti, MI: HighScope Press

3 Active learning

This chapter describes the positive impact of active learning as the *central* principle of the HighScope curriculum, to which every other element interrelates and interconnects. It addresses the theories supporting active learning, including Piaget, Erikson and Vygotsky; and how HighScope has applied theory concisely to all areas of practice, using the five ingredients of active learning. Finally it looks at the KDIs, which are readily apparent in children's active learning and form the HighScope curriculum content.

The centrality of active learning

HighScope uses the term 'active participatory learning' to emphasize the sense of children as constructors of their own knowledge. Active participatory learning is defined as 'learning in which the child, by acting on objects and interacting with people, ideas and events, constructs new understanding. No one else can have experiences for the child or construct knowledge for the child. Children must do this for themselves' (Hohmann, Weikart and Epstein, 2008 p. 17). Young children are natural learners with an innate desire to explore and discover new concepts, they learn by doing and by action. For this reason HighScope practitioners *work with* children rather than *do to* them.

Although not new terminology now, the concept of active learning was ahead of its time in the 1960s, and still so in the 1980s, when HighScope was introduced into the UK; it is now widely accepted as a key principle in early childhood education. In their search for a high-quality

Figure 3.1 The HighScope Wheel of Learning with Active Learning section highlighted

Source: Hohmann, Weikart and Epstein (2008, p. 6)

curriculum as the foundation for the Perry Preschool research project, HighScope teachers and researchers decided to make active learning the *central* element that drives every other aspect of the curriculum (see Chapter 2). It is this decision that is key to understanding the success of the approach because, with training, practice and commitment, the Wheel of Learning (see Chapter 2) provides a thoroughly co-ordinated and coherent framework for practice. This makes it clear that active learning is the driving force behind successful implementation of the HighScope approach.

Theories supporting active learning

Jean Piaget 1896–1980

The original notion of active learning was taken from the work of the child development theorist Jean Piaget (Mooney, 2000 p. 61), 'active' implying interaction and 'learning' implying how children construct knowledge. Learning is seen as a process in which we learn by relating and adding new information to what we already know, and if necessary even changing the way we thought before. The four terms Piaget used to describe this developmental change are:

- *disequilibrium*: a state of intellectual imbalance, a problem provides the motivation to find a solution
- *assimilation:* trying to fit new input into an existing mental framework
- *accommodation:* modifying one's existing mental framework to accept new input, there is a need for change
- *equilibrium:* a state of intellectual balance, inner contentment; the solution to the problem results in new understanding.

The translation of Piaget's theory into practice means that providing moderately novel challenges and problem-solving opportunities will support the breadth of children's learning. Piaget described the need for preschool children to have concrete and active experiences before they are ready for abstract and passive learning. He described several ways of knowing as *sensorimotor, preoperational, concrete operations* and *formal operations* which track children's reasoning and thinking in stages.

1. Sensorimotor stage (0–2½ years)
   Babies and toddlers learn by forming close attachments with primary caregivers and by exploring people, objects and space using all their senses and their whole bodies.
2. Preoperational stage (2½–6 years)
   Children continue to learn through experiences with objects. Thinking is more intuitive than logical; they can now form mental images; they can understand and use language.
3. Concrete operational stage (6–14 years)
   Children can now demonstrate concrete logical thinking, using physical objects to confirm their ideas.

4. Formal operational stage (11–14 years and through to adulthood)
   Children now have the ability to control variables and think beyond
   concrete reality, for instance to think about abstract ideas, propositions
   and hypotheses.

Just listening to children gives a good indication of the need for young
children to have first-hand experiences. A child saying 'I want to share by
myself' is not meant to be cute, but just illustrates his literal inter-
pretations. It shows where he is in child development terms and how his
thinking and reasoning differ from adult thinking. Young children are
learning to put their observations, thoughts and feelings into words. This
is a serious business for them. Words have very concrete, literal meanings
related to actions or things they have directly experienced. To this child
'share', an abstract term, means 'play'; he is interpreting words con-
cretely.

Erik Erikson 1902–94

Erik Erikson, a psychoanalyst from the 1950s, described children's emotional and social development as a series of stages, with *initiative* as the
main task of preschoolers.

Initiative in this context describes children's desire and ability to
follow through on a task. They are motivated from within to do something they want to do, rather than to please someone else. This distinction between intrinsic and extrinsic motivation denotes two opposing
approaches to learning, constructivist and behaviourist (Kohn 1993) (see
Chapter 1, page 10 and Chapter 6, pages 120–2), which are often not
widely recognised in early years practice. Motivation theorists suggest
that children choose to become engaged in activities and interactions that
are enjoyable, are related to their current interests and allow them to
experience feelings of control, success and competence. The ingredients
of active learning (see pages 37–8) provide these conditions, which fire
up children's inner enthusiasm. Educational excellence comes from
intrinsic motivation. The following five factors are central to intrinsic
motivation and HighScope practitioners keep them in mind as they plan
both adult- and child-initiated experiences for children:

■ enjoyment
■ control
■ interest

- probability of success
- feelings of competence and self-confidence.

Lev Vygotsky 1896–1934

Lev Vygotsky (Mooney, 2000 pp. 81–95) saw the social or cultural environment as being particularly crucial to the development of language and thought processes. He referred to the 'zone of proximal development' as the area between what children can accomplish on their own and what they can do with the help of an adult or another child who is more developmentally advanced. Many HighScope teaching practices, particularly the notion that development occurs within sociocultural settings where practitioners scaffold children's learning, were first derived from Vygotsky's work. HighScope practitioners observe children carefully, so they know when and how to enter this zone to scaffold learning to the next level. Children must be secure and confident in what they already know before they are ready to move to the next level. Vygotsky's theories have supported HighScope in achieving a balance between letting children discover for themselves and helping to guide the course of their learning without being either laissez-faire or directive. In HighScope scaffolding means to both:

- support children's current levels of development and
- provide gentle extensions as they move on to the next developmental stage (see Chapter 6, pages 118–19).

The five ingredients of active participatory learning

Active learning is defined by five ingredients which describe the practicalities of how opportunities are provided to support young children's learning in action. These five ingredients are:

1. Choice – The child chooses what to do. Since learning results from the child's attempts to pursue personal interests and goals, the opportunity to choose activities and materials is essential.
2. Materials – There are abundant age-appropriate materials that the child can use in a variety of ways. Learning grows out of the child's direct actions on the materials.

3. Manipulation – The child has opportunities to explore, manipulate, combine and transform the materials chosen.
4. Child language and thought – The child communicates verbally and non-verbally, describing what he or she is seeing and doing. The child reflects on actions, integrating new experiences into existing knowledge, and modifies his or her thinking accordingly.
5. Adult scaffolding – Adults support the child's current level of thinking and challenge the child to advance his or her abilities to reason, problem-solve and create.

Essential Ingredients of Active Learning: A Summary

Choice: The child chooses what to do.
— Children initiate activities that grow from personal interests and intentions.
— Children choose materials.
— Children decide what to do with materials.

Materials: There are abundant materials that children can use in many ways.
— Children use a variety of materials.
  — Practical everyday objects
  — Natural and found materials
  — Tools
  — Messy, sticky, gooey, drippy, squishy materials
  — Heavy, large materials
  — Easy-to-handle materials
— Children have space to use materials.
— Children have time to use materials.

Manipulation: Adults encourage children to manipulate objects freely.
— Children explore actively with all their senses.
— Children discover relationships through direct experience.
— Children transform and combine materials.
— Children use age-appropriate tools and equipment.
— Children use their large muscles.

Child language and thought: The child describes what he or she is thinking and doing.
— Children talk about their experiences.
— Children talk about what they are doing in their own words.

Adult scaffolding: Adults recognize and encourage children's intentions, reflections, problem solving, and creativity.
— Adults form partnerships with children.
  — Put themselves on children's physical level.
  — Follow children's ideas and interests.
  — Converse in a give-and-take style.
— Adults seek out children's intentions.
  — Acknowledge children's choices and actions.
  — Use materials in the same way children are using them.
  — Watch what children do with materials.
  — Ask children about their intentions.
— Adults listen for and encourage children's thinking.
  — Listen to children as they work and play.
  — Converse with children about what they are doing and thinking.
  — Focus on children's actions.
  — Make comments that repeat, amplify, and build on what the child says.
  — Pause frequently to give children time to think and gather their thoughts into words.
  — Accept children's answers and explanations even when they are "wrong".
— Adults encourage children to do things for themselves.
  — Stand by patiently and wait while children take care of things independently.
  — Show understanding of children's mishaps.
  — Refer children to one another for ideas, assistance, and conversation.
  — Encourage children to ask and answer their own questions.

Figure 3.2 Essential ingredients of active learning: a summary

Source: Hohmann, Weikart and Epstein (2008, p.40)

In the HighScope curriculum, the ingredients of active participatory learning guide every experience and activity that adults and children engage in during their time together. This could be in a formally structured day or as part of other daily events such as trips in a car or visits to a park. They are used by practitioners as a tool to evaluate whether an activity for children is truly a developmentally appropriate, active experience and to plan for activities that meet these criteria.

Box 3.1 Analysing a five-minute observation of *Star Wars* play using the five ingredients of active participatory learning

Context

At work time (child-initiated play) in the building area. Four boys aged 4 years: Jules, Elvis, Yusei and Benjamin.

 During planning time Jules and Elvis decided to bring the wooden door and window frame out into the building area so they could make a 'Star Wars' house. Once they had completed this task Yusei and Benjamin came over and wanted to play.

Benjamin: "What are you playing?"
Jules: "Star Wars, but we need robots."
Benjamin: "I can help build robots."
Yusei: "Yeah, me too."
Practitioner: "What will you use to build the robots?"
Benjamin: "Big Lego"
Jules, Elvis and Yusei in unison: "Yeah, big Lego."

 They all go over and pull the two big plastic containers of Lego over to the building area and bring it inside the house. They begin to take turns putting the Lego into place, starting with a big square base and then going narrow as they get higher.

Yusei: "I can't reach it."
Benjamin: "Get a chair."
Elvis: "I need a chair too."
Jules: "Hey R2D2 doesn't have eyes. Take this Lego off." He points to the Lego with a painted eye on it. "And he needs arms."
Elvis: "These arms here!" He found two paper towel rolls and held them up.
Yusei: "They don't fit on the Lego."

Practitioner: "How else could you attach the arms to the Lego?"
Benjamin: "Tape, I'll get it." He goes to the art area and brings back the tape dispenser.

The robot is not finished, so the tape is put down and the robot is made higher and higher. It falls over three times, and three times they fix it. When it falls again Jules shouts "That's it, R2D2 got blown up by the bad guys."

Then they cleaned up and decided to build a spaceship out of the Lego that they could all sit on.

Practitioner's analysis

Choice
The boys had complete choice for their work-time activity. Once they all agreed on what their goal was (to play Star Wars and make the robot R2D2) they looked around the classroom and had a choice between large Lego, small Lego, blocks and other materials to begin their task. They spotted the large and colourful Lego and decided to use these building materials to start. I feel they chose the Lego because of its colours, the easy fitting design and because it was large and would feel more 'size appropriate' for the robot.

Materials
The boys were able to use pre-made props in the classroom to start their play and then, with a question from the practitioner, they were able to create props from the other materials in the classroom. There was plenty of big Lego for four boys to play with and work together to create a robot. When the problem of arms and how to attach them came up, once again one of the boys found the arms in the collage box and the other boy was easily able to bring tape from the art area to help complete their idea. The availability of the materials allowed the boys to extend their play, add details and find solutions to their problems.

Manipulation
Each of the boys used some type of material or object in a way that was helpful to their mission of building the robot. When it got too high, they brought in a chair to manage the height difference and add more Lego. They were going to use kitchen paper rolls as arms and tape to apply them. They also brought out the 'outline' of their play with the wooden door and window frame as their spaceship. It was inside this 'outlined' space that all the building began. They had the time and space to explore and use the materials.

Child language and thought
The boys seemed to be able to express their ideas, problems, solutions and needs in very clear sentences. Each child's ideas, needs or solutions were acknowledged by the other children or the adult. And when the play was over, there was general acceptance because Jules explained his idea of what had happened to the robot, and it was a logical explanation and accepted by all the other children playing.

Adult scaffolding
The practitioner stepped in only to seek clarification and to further their solution to a problem by asking an open-ended question. Her two questions encouraged the boys to decide on building materials and to think of other ways to solve the problem of attaching arms to the robot by using other available material.

Figure 3.3
Star Wars
play (photo:
A. Madeira)

Key developmental indicators – the HighScope curriculum content for under-threes

While active learning provides the *process* of the HighScope approach, KDIs provide the *content* by which we can measure the progress of active learning as it takes place. There are 42 KDIs in six curriculum areas for under-threes. The KDIs are early childhood milestones that guide practitioners as they plan and assess learning experiences and interact with children to support learning. Each KDI is a guideline that identifies an observable behaviour typical of children under three, reflecting knowledge and skills in the areas of approaches to learning; social and emotional development; physical development and health; communication, language and literacy; cognitive development; and creative arts. A list of the KDIs for under-threes follows.

Box 3.2 Key developmental indicators for under-threes

A. Approaches to learning

1. *Initiative:* Children express initiative.
2. *Problem-solving:* Children solve problems encountered in exploration and play.
3. *Self-help:* Children do things for themselves.

B. Social and emotional development

4. *Distinguishing self and others:* Children distinguish themselves from others.
5. *Attachment:* Children form an attachment to a primary caregiver.
6. *Relationships with adults:* Children build relationships with other adults.
7. *Relationships with peers:* Children build relationships with peers.
8. *Emotions:* Children express emotions.
9. *Empathy:* Children show empathy toward the feelings and needs of others.
10. *Playing with others:* Children play with others.
11. *Group participation:* Children participate in group routines.

C. Physical development and health

12. *Moving parts of the body:* Children move parts of the body (turning head, grasping, kicking).

---

13. *Moving the whole body:* Children move the whole body (rolling, crawling, cruising, walking, running, balancing).
14. *Moving with objects:* Children move with objects.
15. *Steady beat:* Children feel and experience steady beat.

D. Communication, language, and literacy

16. *Listening and responding:* Children listen and respond.
17. *Nonverbal communication:* Children communicate non-verbally.
18. *Two-way communication:* Children participate in two-way communication.
19. *Speaking:* Children speak.
20. *Exploring print:* Children explore picture books and magazines.
21. *Enjoying language:* Children enjoy stories, rhymes and songs.

E. Cognitive development

22. *Exploring objects:* Children explore objects with their hands, feet, mouth, eyes, ears and nose.
23. *Object permanence:* Children discover object permanence.
24. *Exploring same and different:* Children explore and notice how things are the same or different.
25. *Exploring more:* Children experience 'more'.
26. *One-to-one correspondence:* Children experience one-to-one correspondence.
27. *Number:* Children experience the number of things.
28. *Locating objects:* Children explore and notice the location of objects.
29. *Filling and emptying:* Children fill and empty, put in and take out.
30. *Taking apart and putting together:* Children take things apart and fit them together.
31. *Seeing from different viewpoints:* Children observe people and things from various perspectives.
32. *Anticipating events:* Children anticipate familiar events.
33. *Time intervals:* Children notice the beginning and ending of time intervals.
34. *Speed:* Children experience 'fast' and 'slow'.
35. *Cause and effect:* Children repeat an action to make something happen again, experience cause and effect.

F. Creative arts

36. *Imitating and pretending:* Children imitate and pretend.
37. *Exploring art materials:* Children explore building and art materials.
38. *Identifying visual images:* Children respond to and identify pictures and photographs.

39. *Listening to music:* Children listen to music.
40. *Responding to music:* Children respond to music.
41. *Sounds:* Children explore and imitate sounds.
42. *Vocal pitch:* Children explore vocal pitch sounds.

Key developmental indicators – the HighScope curriculum content for preschool children

The preschool KDIs are a series of statements that form a curriculum for social, cognitive and physical development of children from the ages of 3 to 5 years. Each statement highlights a type of active child behaviour that is essential for the development of the fundamental abilities that emerge during early childhood. The KDIs are not a set of specific topics and learning objectives; instead they are basic concepts and skills that young children naturally use repeatedly, given the opportunity. Together, the KDIs define the kind of knowledge young children are acquiring as they interact with materials, people, ideas and events.

Since the KDIs describe activities that young children readily engage in, the role of the adult is to create environments in which these behaviours can occur and then to recognise, support and build on them when they do. HighScope KDIs are organised around the following topics:

■ approaches to learning
■ social and emotional development
■ physical development and health
■ language, literacy and communication
■ mathematics
■ creative arts
■ science and technology
■ social studies.

The KDIs are used to guide daily planning, guide observations of children, enable adults to see things from a child's point of view and help to audit materials and room arrangement as well as the daily routine.

Put simply, the reason active participatory learning works is because it matches what children *want* to do (initiative) with what they *need* to do (KDIs).

Box 3.3 Key developmental indicators for preschoolers

A. Approaches to learning

1. **Initiative:** Children demonstrate initiative as they explore their world.
2. **Planning:** Children make plans and follow through on their intentions.
3. **Engagement:** Children focus on activities that interest them.
4. **Problem solving:** Children solve problems encountered in play.
5. **Use of resources:** Children gather information and formulate ideas about their world.
6. **Reflection:** Children reflect on their experiences.

B. Social and emotional development

7. **Self-identity:** Children have a positive self-identity.
8. **Sense of competence:** Children feel they are competent.
9. **Emotions:** Children recognize, label, and regulate their feelings.
10. **Empathy:** Children demonstrate empathy toward others.
11. **Community:** Children participate in the community of the classroom.
12. **Building relationships:** Children build relationships with other children and adults.
13. **Cooperative play:** Children engage in cooperative play.
14. **Moral development:** Children develop an internal sense of right and wrong.
15. **Conflict resolution:** Children resolve social conflicts.

C. Physical development and health

16. **Gross-motor skills:** Children demonstrate strength, flexibility, balance, and timing in using their large muscles.
17. **Fine-motor skills:** Children demonstrate dexterity and hand-eye coordination in using their small muscles.
18. **Body awareness:** Children know about their bodies and how to navigate them in space.
19. **Personal care:** Children carry out personal care routines on their own.
20. **Healthy behavior:** Children engage in healthy practices.

D. Language, literacy, and communication[1]

21. **Comprehension:** Children understand language.
22. **Speaking:** Children express themselves using language.
23. **Vocabulary:** Children understand and use a variety of words and phrases.
24. **Phonological awareness:** Children identify distinct sounds in spoken language.

25. **Alphabetic knowledge:** Children identify letter names and their sounds.
26. **Reading:** Children read for pleasure and information.
27. **Concepts about print:** Children demonstrate knowledge about environmental print.
28. **Book knowledge:** Children demonstrate knowledge about books.
29. **Writing:** Children write for many different purposes.
30. **ELL/Dual language acquisition:** (If applicable) Children use English and their home language(s) (including sign language).

E. Mathematics

31. **Number words and symbols:** Children recognize and use number words and symbols.
32. **Counting:** Children count things.
33. **Part-whole relationships:** Children combine and separate quantities of objects.
34. **Shapes:** Children identify, name, and describe shapes.
35. **Spatial awareness:** Children recognize spatial relationships among people and objects.
36. **Measuring:** Children measure to describe, compare, and order things.
37. **Unit:** Children understand and use the concept of unit.
38. **Patterns:** Children identify, describe, copy, complete, and create patterns.
39. **Data analysis:** Children use information about quantity to draw conclusions, make decisions, and solve problems.

F. Creative arts

40. **Art:** Children express and represent what they observe, think, imagine, and feel through two- and three-dimensional art.
41. **Music:** Children express and represent what they observe, think, imagine, and feel through music.
42. **Movement:** Children express and represent what they observe, think, imagine, and feel through movement.
43. **Pretend play:** Children express and represent what they observe, think, imagine, and feel through pretend play.
44. **Appreciating the arts:** Children appreciate the creative arts.

G. Science and Technology

45. **Observing:** Children observe the materials and processes in their environment.
46. **Classifying:** Children classify materials, actions, people, and events.

47. **Experimenting:** Children experiment to test their ideas.
48. **Predicting:** Children predict what they expect will happen.
49. **Drawing conclusions:** Children draw conclusions based on their experiences and observations.
50. **Communicating ideas:** Children communicate their ideas about the characteristics of things and how they work.
51. **Natural and physical world:** Children gather knowledge about the natural and physical world.
52. **Tools and technology:** Children explore and use tools and technology.

H. Social studies

53. **Diversity:** Children understand that people have diverse characteristics, interests, and abilities.
54. **Community roles:** Children recognize that people have different roles and functions in the community.
55. **Decision making:** Children participate in making classroom decisions.
56. **Geography:** Children recognize and interpret features and locations in their environment.
57. **History:** Children understand past, present, and future.
58. **Ecology:** Children understand the importance of taking care of their environment.

---

1 Language, Literacy, and Communication KDIs 21–29 may be used for the child's home language(s) as well as English. KDI 30 refers specifically to ELL/Dual language acquisition.

HighScope is currently updating the KDIs based on the latest research in child development and effective teaching practices. For updates to the KDIs, visit the website: http://www.highscope.org/Content.asp?ContentId=566.

Active learning in support of family involvement

The ingredients of active-learning choice, materials, manipulation, child language and adult scaffolding – guide HighScope's approach not only to children but also to families. When children make choices about what to play and how to use materials, they will often make choices that reflect experiences they have had at home, like how to make tea and important family situations such as weddings. Children are very powerfully motivated to imitate parents and family members, so practitioners will provide materials that children are familiar with from home to manipulate. They will also add carefully selected pictures, books and magazines so that children will see images of families like their own. Practitioners will encourage language from children in many ways, such as welcoming children's talk about their home experiences, hiring staff who speak the children's home languages and, if they don't speak those languages, taking the time to learn important words and phrases so that children and family members feel comfortable communicating with them. Finally, they will scaffold children's learning by building on the experiences the children bring from home and by helping parents to extend education from the classroom to the family environment.

HighScope practitioners find that active learning is an adventure, and they do not always know exactly where the children will take them. It contains the optimal balance between the need for children to explore and discover and the need to ensure their safety and well-being. When all five ingredients of active participatory learning are present it leads to mature, purposeful play with high-order thinking, independence, initiative and problem-solving; skills for life-long learning.

Key points

1. Active learning is defined as learning in which the child, by acting on objects and interacting with people, ideas and events, constructs new understanding.
2. Active learning is the central principle of the HighScope approach which drives every other element of the curriculum, and this results in a fully coherent approach.
3. The HighScope curriculum is grounded in child development theory.
4. To understand the practical application of active learning, HighScope defines five essential ingredients: choice, materials, manipulation, child language and thought and adult scaffolding.
5. Active learning works because when all five ingredients are present children are busy and focused, and they are personally motivated in their endeavours.
6. The challenge for HighScope practitioners is to keep the ingredients of active learning in mind throughout all parts of the daily routine and use them to plan for and evaluate activities.

7. With active learning, HighScope focuses first on the process of learning – how young children learn; when this is in place, the content – what young children learn – occurs naturally.
8. The KDIs provide the content by which the progress of active learning is measured and related to the content frameworks of statutory early years frameworks in different countries.
9. Active learning works because it matches what children *want* to do (initiative) with what they *need* to do (KDIs).
10. The process of active learning leads to dispositions such as initiative, independence, decision making, divergent thinking and problem solving, which can't be directly taught and are skills for life-long learning.

Reflections on the HighScope approach

1. Active learning
   ■ Are HighScope's five ingredients of active learning present during your child-initiated activities?
   ■ Are HighScope's five ingredients of active learning present during your adult-initiated activities?
2. Intrinsic motivation
   ■ What are your children doing when they are fully engaged in activities?
   ■ What does this tell you about meaningful learning activities?
   ■ What conditions are present when you are absorbed in work or hobbies?
3. Children's thinking and reasoning
   ■ Can you share an example of children's literal thinking, for example "I want to share by myself"?
   ■ What does this tell you about child development and how best to support learning?
4. Dispositions for learning
   ■ What dispositions do you think are important for life-long learning?
   ■ What do you do in your setting to support them?
5. Key developmental indicators
   ■ How is the content of your curriculum defined?
   ■ In what ways do you use this to guide your work?
   ■ How easy would it be to map the content of your curriculum against the KDIs?

References

Hohmann, M., Weikart, D. & Epstein, A. (2008) "Active Participatory Learning, the way children construct knowledge", Part 1 Chapter 1, and "Curriculum Development in Early Childhood Development", Part 3 Chapters 9–22 in *Educating Young Children*. Ypsilanti, MI: HighScope Press

Kohn, A. (1993) *Punished by Rewards*. Boston: Houghton Mifflin

Mooney, C. (2000) *Theories of Childhood: An introduction to Dewey, Montessori, Erikson, Piaget and Vygotsky*. Minnesota: Redleaf Press

Related reading

Epstein, A. (2007) "What is the HighScope Preschool Curriculum?", Chapter 2, pp. 7–14, and "What is the Theory behind the HighScope Curriculum?", Chapter 3, pp 15–20 in *Essentials of Active Learning in Preschool: Getting to Know the HighScope Curriculum*. Ypsilanti, MI: HighScope Press

Post, J., Hohmann, M., & Epstein, A. S. (2011) *Tender Care and Early Learning: Supporting Infants and Toddlers in Child Care Settings* (2nd edn). Ypsilanti, MI: HighScope Press

4 The learning environment

This chapter describes the thoughtful organisation of space for active learners by looking at the practical details of interest areas, storage and materials. It highlights the hallmarks of labelling, accessible storage, a balance of commercial and free and found materials and display seen in HighScope settings, and how similar principles apply in the outdoor learning environment and settings for under-threes. The use of space is exemplified by descriptions of two visits to HighScope settings, one to an under-threes unit in a purpose-built preschool and one to a preschool room in a Victorian house.

We are all influenced by places, and attention to the detail of an aesthetically pleasing environment is important for children and practitioners alike. A sense of emotional tone can be achieved by lighting (both natural and artificial), colour, textures, furnishing, plants and sounds.

The most important principle of the HighScope learning environment is that children should be able to find, use and return the materials they need on their own.

Every HighScope setting will be different in terms of space, lay-out and design, but all HighScope settings are recognisable by an organised, uncluttered look and certain characteristics such as low-level accessible storage and labelling. They will be easy for new adults and children alike to find their way around. The room arrangement gives many unspoken messages about the approach to education, and the way materials are organised makes a significant difference to their learning value.

As a key element in the process of learning, the learning environment is the context for active learning, and practitioners aim to make the most effective use of their space so that children can be independent, use their initiative and make choices.

Figure 4.1 The HighScope Wheel of Learning with the Learning Environment section highlighted

Source: Hohmann, Weikart and Epstein (2008, p. 6)

The five ingredients of active learning (Chapter 3) give a useful introduction to the rationale and guidelines that HighScope practitioners use for arranging and equipping spaces for children. Storage will be visible and accessible so that children can see the *choices* available and easily reach the materials. *Materials* will be of interest and inviting for children to explore, transform and combine. They will be arranged to promote *manipulation*, children's direct use of materials, as opposed to being arranged primarily for demonstration or display. There will be interesting things to talk about, promoting *child language and thought*, and room for adults to watch and comfortably join children's play, providing *adult scaffolding*.

As the Wheel of Learning shows the thoughtful organisation of space is implemented in HighScope settings by paying particular attention to:

- interest areas
- storage
- materials.

The HighScope learning environment for under-threes

In HighScope settings the learning environment for under-threes provides children with a sense of comfort and well-being and at the same time provides ample opportunity for active learning. Its organisation follows the same principles as for preschool children but is distinguished to match the developmental needs of the youngest children, the need for space to crawl, balance and walk and the need for distinct areas for eating, sleeping, bodily care and play.

Interest areas

With defined areas for eating, sleeping and bodily care, the rest of the space in the setting is devoted to exploration and play. In HighScope settings non-mobile babies have a defined safe space to lie or sit. This may be in a fixed location or may be defined by a large blanket or quilt and moved to provide babies with different things to look at. Toddlers play in appealing interest areas to meet their needs as sensory-motor active learners (Chapter 3), exploring and discovering using all their senses and their increasing mobility. The consistency in their environment allows them to return again and again to familiar things and experiences. The interest areas will include the art area, house area, book area and block area. If space permits, other desirable areas for toddlers include a movement area where they can run, climb, rock and ride and a toy area where they can engage in putting things together and taking them apart, filling and emptying and pretending.

In arranging the play space, practitioners are mindful to include ample space for toddlers to move about, to use materials and to have social interaction, but are also aware of the importance of 'nooks and crannies' or private space to rest, observe and recharge emotionally. Comfortable adult seating, where children and adults can be cosy, supports this psychological necessity.

Storage

Non-mobile babies have a portable storage system of small baskets, boxes, buckets, cloth bags and tins containing appealing sensory materials which practitioners take to wherever the baby is lying or sitting. For toddlers, storage is low level and accessible, with particular attention paid to immovable and untippable shelves for toddlers who hang on to them to pull themselves up to stand. Practitioners make professional judgements on which materials are stored at a high level and used only in small group time under close supervision to ensure children's safety – for example, items like scissors and glue.

Individual 'cubbies' are available to store pleasant reminders from home, such as comfort blankets or soft toys and a small, easy-to-handle album of family photos.

Labelling for toddlers is distinguished by using the most 'concrete' form of representation, using the actual object, photograph, picture or outline.

Materials

Babies take great interest in everyday materials and 'treasure baskets' containing natural and real objects like tins, large pebbles, chains, a lemon, costume jewellery, woollen balls and wooden spoons are available in HighScope settings. In addition to a balance of open-ended, real, free and found and commercial materials, practitioners pay particular attention to supporting young children's sensory-motor approach to learning because babies and toddlers are eager to explore and learn directly, using their whole body and all their senses. HighScope settings for under-threes have aromatic materials and experiences, sound-producing materials and experiences, materials to touch, mouth, taste and look at. They also include space and materials that support the movement tasks very young children are striving to master, with things to climb on and jump off, things to get inside of, pull and push toys and balls.

Box 4.1 A visit to an under-threes' unit in a purpose-built preschool

This under-threes' unit in a purpose-built preschool was renovated in 2008. It comprises the home base for two 13-place toddler rooms for children aged between 1 and 3 years, a shared kitchen, changing area, children's and staff toilets, cloakroom, two storage rooms and a staff room.

The two toddler rooms are arranged to serve both as individual rooms for designated groups of children and as a shared space with a connecting door at choice time, the child-initiated period of the day. This gives the toddlers more space and play opportunities. Both rooms are characterised by distinct interest areas bordered by low-level wooden storage units, which are on castors to facilitate cleaning underneath. The rooms are called Bunnies classroom and Pandas classroom. Both rooms have a building area, movement area, book area, art area and pretending area, but because the rooms are not a mirror image, Pandas classroom has a large kitchen area and Bunnies has a larger art area and book area. To avoid repetition, this account focuses on the Bunnies classroom.

The central and largest area is the *building area*, where children and practitioners can gather together at greeting time or large group time. This area is characterised by a circle on the floor containing each child's photo and a picture of an animal chosen by the child and covered with contact film. This is used as a transition strategy for the children to find their 'spot' to sit on at greeting time and large group time. On the wall in this area is the daily routine chart – a line of photographs and words describing the order of the day, for example greeting time, large group time, snack time and so forth. The storage unit facing the building area houses Duplo Lego, bricks and train tracks. At choice time there is ample space for building and small-world play without interference from the shopping trolleys and buggies that are housed in the neighbouring *movement area* along with small cars, trucks and balls. Opposite is the *pretending area*, which has a shop front and accessible storage for scarves, bags, hats, recycled toiletries, phones, cameras and musical instruments. During choice time Pamela and Hyewon put scarves on their heads and create a two-part dance, involving stomping and twirling, which they repeat several times.

The *art area* is the only interest area with a table and chairs, so there is the maximum amount of available floor space. Storage includes pots of felt-tip pens, crayons and pipe cleaners, and in the wooden storage unit an art box for finished two-dimensional art work, white paper, coloured paper, play dough, collage materials and pegs. On the wall there is a whiteboard and in the corner a sand or water tray. On this visit there are eight children around the table drawing, but then three children become absorbed by clipping pegs first around the edges of paper and then on the edges of their sleeves.

Bordering the art area is the *book area*. This area is made to feel cosy, with a red sofa which can seat five children. Books are housed in a wall rack and the storage unit houses home-made 'shakers', stacking containers, shaker blocks and stacking boxes. There is also netting storage for soft toys to cuddle and play with.

Each of the interest areas is clearly labelled so it is easy to find your way around, and materials are labelled in a standard way using a photograph and the word. This and a minimalist yet 'enough materials' policy gives an organised look to the room and aids tidy-up time. Materials are rotated according to children's prevailing interests and the time of year, using stock from a well-resourced storage room along the corridor.

As several children are in nappies, there is a changing room with windows overlooking the Pandas classroom. This has two small portable step ladders to a purpose-built changing area with two changing mats and a sink in between. This has been designed to minimise the institutional feel of the toddler unit. There is a sliding nappy storage unit for each child, labelled with both the classroom logo and the child's photograph. Along the corridor there is a child's toilet, hand basin with accessible soap and hand towels and bin for the older toddlers to use.

Just outside the two classrooms the corridor houses wooden storage drawers for each child to store their rest-time blanket, pillow and any comforters, as well as photographs of their family which children sometimes take to their rest time. Above these drawers, which are labelled with the class logo and child's photo, are each child's portfolio of anecdotal observations and samples of work. These are accessible to parents and children at any time. On the wall outside each classroom is a whiteboard and corkboard. The whiteboard is for daily information, including a brief account of what the children did at large group time, small group time and choice time and a photo of things happening during the day. The corkboard is for the weekly newsletter, the weekly menu and a simple sleeping and eating report for parents to see. Further along the corridor are a wall-sized car and bus with child-sized seats used as a transition strategy, along with a wavy mirror and other wall activities to keep children active during waiting periods. There is wall space for Bunnies and Pandas classrooms art display.

There is a separate kitchen space for this 26-place under-threes unit. The children have their lunch and afternoon snack in here, seated at five round tables. There are six high chairs, from which children move on when they are able to sit safely on the adult-sized chairs with a child-height foot bar. Each chair is labelled with the child's picture and classroom logo. Lunches are prepared off the premises and the kitchen is equipped with a fridge, freezer, microwave and oven for snacks and an industrial dish washer. There are a child-accessible hand sink, soap dispenser and paper towel dispenser.

With its own access to the outdoor learning environment, there is a substantial cloakroom with a storage rack to house each child's outdoor clothing, a see-through box for gloves and hat, a rack for shoes and a mobile wellington-boot holder. In the cloakroom there are also a drying cupboard and individual parents' post boxes.

The outdoor space is shared with neighbouring apartments, with the pre-school area fenced off. Within the preschool area there is fixed equipment, including a swing, slide and climbing frame, boat and house. The house is in the centre of a large sand area. There is a storage room for loose materials, including bats, balls, hoops, wheeled toys and recycled materials like logs and fir cones.

This visit took place in the winter and the children built a volcano out of snow; pretended to be reindeer pulling each other on sledges; and scraped up the ice and snow into a see-through jar to observe what happened when it was taken indoors. Three-year-old Noah exclaimed when pulling the sledge: "It's like a roller coaster!" The children have the sole use of the outdoor space for an hour every day, so the playground is not crowded, and the children also have a scheduled outing once a week.

Environments for preschool children

Interest areas

HighScope settings are divided into interest areas. These are defined by the kinds of play young children enjoy – sensory exploration, building, creating things, pretending, using books and playing simple games – as opposed to content areas like communication, language and literacy and personal, social and emotional development. In any HighScope setting there will be four essential areas: the art area, house area, book area and block and small world area. These areas are prioritised to meet the HighScope philosophy of intrinsic motivation, that is, children will play and learn in these areas because they want to (Chapter 3). Universally the areas reflect the kinds of play young children engage in. If space permits, the setting may also have other desirable areas, for example, the computer area, music and movement area and woodwork area. However, each setting will use a common language to describe these areas so that they are simple to understand and make sense to children. For example, the art area may be known as the 'make and do' area, the home area as the 'pretending area' and the construction area as the 'connecting area'. In addition, the names may have a cultural dimension – in Sweden the house area is called the kitchen area. In all centre-based settings the space available is for children and the activities that adults share with them;

this means that other non-play equipment and supplies are located else-where.

The areas in the setting are defined by low boundaries which can include low shelves, storage boxes, tape or rugs so children can see everywhere. To identify the purpose of an area each one is labelled with a large sign, at least A4 size. This may display an actual object found in that area, a picture of the materials or activities typical of the area and the written name of the area. For example, children might see a real paint brush or a large drawing of a crayon and the words 'Art Area' on a sign labelling that part of the room. This system allows children at various stages of literacy development to comprehend the labels and practise literacy skills.

Location

By observing children at play, practitioners determine the best location for areas, taking into account permanent fixtures like radiators, doors, sinks and floor coverings. For example, since children often use materials from the block and small world area in the house area and vice versa, these two areas are often located next to or near one another. Practitioners monitor the use of spaces so that if one area is particularly popular it will be enlarged, or if an area is not being used it will be revitalised or reintro-duced through an adult-initiated activity.

Each area is organised to provide enough space for materials and for as many children as want to play there. Adults do not limit the number of children who can use a given area at any time because doing so restricts children's freedom to make choices, pursue their interests and learn to resolve conflicts over space and materials. This supports the HighScope philosophy of shared control between children and adults, and problem solving. Although materials are arranged by area, children are free to carry materials from one area to another and materials will be returned to their correct area at tidy-up time.

In HighScope settings the room arrangement remains consistent, pro-viding a sense of security and control for children. This means that children do not have to wait for, or depend on, practitioners in order to achieve their goals. In the interest areas the materials children enjoy using are available every day, rather than being set out only on certain days, and children know they can always use materials they want to use again. This consistent and regular arrangement of materials and equip-ment promotes self-confidence and independent problem solving.

Flexibility

As the design and lay-out of every HighScope setting is different, flexibility and common sense is applied to the location of interest areas to meet the needs of active learners. In settings with adjoining rooms the children often come together at 'work time' (Chapter 5) so that fewer but richer interest areas are provided. In settings without separate rooms for eating and resting, practitioners take particular care to ensure that potential interest areas are not filled up with tables that are used only for eating. In some settings the block area doubles up as a space large enough for group meetings. Older children help to organise the environment, and make their own labels to identify the areas and materials stored there.

In home-based settings art areas are usually in the kitchen or garden, landings can be used for block and small world areas and the space between two armchairs in the living room can be used to create a space for 'pretending'. Settings that share space with other users or family members make good use of wheeled boxes and furnishings, stacking boxes, hinged storage units that close up and display boards.

Storage

Position

Storage is a key consideration in HighScope settings and supports the theme of logical organisation within the interest areas. Similar materials are stored together, the blocks in the block area, the art supplies in the art area and so forth to help children to find and return things they need in their play. Within each interest area, materials with similar functions are placed close together to help children see alternatives and think about different ways of accomplishing tasks. For example, in the art area, the various drawing tools – crayons, markers, chalk, coloured pencils – can be found on one shelf, and fasteners – tape, paper clips, staples, string, wool, glue – are stored on another shelf.

Containers

The types of storage used can vary from recycled to bought containers, the unifying feature being that children can see into and handle them easily. Recycled materials like shoe boxes, cutlery trays, vegetable containers provide highly visible storage for small materials. Vegetable racks, sturdy boxes and milk crates are used to store larger materials. Plastic, wooden and basket containers are used to add a variety of textures to the room. Some large materials like hollow blocks do not need containers and are stored directly on the floor.

Labelling

Attention to labelling is a recognisable feature of a HighScope setting, with a clear rationale supporting the find-use-return cycle, where children find the materials they need to carry out their intentions and put them away afterwards. Labels can be found both on the container and on the shelf where the container is placed, providing a regular storage space where children can find what they need and then return the material, even if it is scattered during play. The labels used are understandable to young children and include those made from the material itself as well as tracings of the material, drawings, catalogue pictures, photographs and photocopies, used along with a word. Picture labels provide a map that children can 'read' on their own. At tidy-up time children enjoy sorting materials into their containers and matching things to their labels on the shelves. They also enjoy deciding where new materials should go and making their own labels for them. Labels are often laminated to make them easy to attach to shelves or containers, more durable and easily moveable when it is time to make room for new materials.

Less is more

Another recognisable feature of a HighScope setting is that 'less is more'. For example, on a puzzle shelf there will be a single line of three or four puzzles rather than many puzzles stacked up just to fit them all in. Whilst the play space may look busy and cluttered during work time (Chapter 5), uncluttered storage makes children's ownership of and responsibility for the learning environment both manageable and a reality.

Personal belongings

In a HighScope setting each child has a personal space where he can keep track of personal belongings, such as clothing or a painting to take home. This can be a drawer, basket or box which is labelled with the child's name and photograph or symbol. This is in addition to a labelled storage

Figure 4.2 Accessible storage (photo: M. Wiltshire)

space for outdoor clothing. Parents comment on how welcoming this is on their child's first day, seeing the storage space for their own child labelled with both a name and a photograph, as well as there being a personal mail box for each parent.

By devoting time and effort to storage, practitioners foster independence, decision making and initiative in young children and create a genuine feeling of belonging for families. This implicit process significantly supports the HighScope philosophy of empowering children and families.

Materials

HighScope settings show that they value children's home and family life by including many items found in the home, such as magazines, books, photographs, dolls, clothing, music and food containers that accurately reflect the cultural and linguistic diversity of the children in the setting.

Equipment and materials can also portray such realities as differences in family make-up and disabilities, so there may be music from home, pretend house pets, books in different languages, work clothes from jobs held by children's parents, crutches and glasses with the lenses removed. In this concrete way children are enabled to feel comfortable and secure as they move between the home and early childhood setting and learning about diversity becomes a natural part of nursery life.

There are no defined materials in HighScope as there are, for example, in the Montessori approach, and in a HighScope setting there will be a balance between commercial and free and found materials. Materials found in each area support a wide range of play suitable to the interests and emerging abilities of the children in the setting. There are:

- materials for sensory exploration, building, making things, pretending and playing simple games
- materials that encourage children's interests in art, music, drama, writing and story-telling, numbers and the physical world
- materials that support children's key developmental indicators in language and literacy, creative representation, social relations, similarities and differences, ordering and patterning, number, space, movement and time.

To support this way of working there are many materials that are fairly simple in themselves but that are open ended and that children can use in many different ways, depending on their interests, abilities and experiences. For example, materials such as balls, blocks, paper and scarves. As well as items made specifically for children, such as toys, puzzles and dolls, there are many real items such as phones, keys, measuring scales and cooking utensils, which add greater authenticity to play and which children often prefer to plastic replicas. There are also natural and recycled items, which enrich creative possibilities and add a useful contrast in texture and colour compared to many purchased plastic items. This enables children to explore and discover the properties of wood, stone, shells, leaves and other natural materials.

Materials are available in sufficient quantities so that children can make an informed choice without having to wait, which also helps to minimise conflicts over who gets to use what, and when. This approach is carefully balanced with having not too much of any one type of material, which can detract from organisation and the use of these materials.

Display

Display in a HighScope setting reflects the ethos of active learning and celebrates children's creativity. There are designated places for both 2D and 3D finished and unfinished work. The display space for finished work is located where it can be easily viewed by children at their eye level, either on the wall, display board or shelf. It may include a label alongside with the child's name, the child's description of the work and any other information the child wants to include.

Unfinished 3D work, either with construction toys like Lego or models made from recycled materials, is kept safe by using a 'work in progress' sign. 'Work in progress' signs validate the importance of children's work, remind them of their on-going projects and invite conversation with peers and adults about their interests and accomplishments.

Ephemeral work (such as chalkmarks on a playground) or creations that will be dismantled so the materials can be reused are permanently recorded and displayed using photographs.

At the end of the day parents will be able to see a brief account of what children did at large group time, small group time and work time, along with a photograph and anecdotes typically displayed on a whiteboard alongside a general parent information board.

Figure 4.3 Work in Progress sign (photo: M. Wiltshire)

Box 4.2 Guidelines and strategies for arranging and equipping spaces for children: A summary

Organising space

— The space is inviting to children. It includes
  — Softness
  — Rounded corners
  — Pleasing colours and textures
  — Natural materials and light
  — Cosy places
— The space is divided into well-defined interest areas to encourage distinctive types of play.
— The interest areas include some combination of the following:
  — Sand and water area
  — Block area
  — House area
  — Art area
  — Toy area
  — Book and writing area
  — Woodworking area
  — Music and movement area
  — Computer area
  — Outdoor area
— The space incorporates places for group activities, eating, resting, and storing children's belongings.

Establishing interest areas

— The interest areas are arranged to promote visibility and easy movement between areas:
  — The sand and water area is close to water.
  — The block and house areas are close to each other.
  — The art area is close to water.
  — The toy and book areas are located away from vigorous play areas.
  — The woodworking area is outdoors or near the art area.
  — The computer area avoids screen glare.
  — The outdoor area is close to indoor areas.
— The areas can accommodate practical considerations and children's changing interests.

Providing materials

— The storage of materials promotes the find-use-return cycle.
  — Similar things are stored together.
  — Children can see into and handle containers.
  — Labels make sense to children. They are made from
    — The materials themselves
    — Photographs, photocopies
    — Pictures
    — Line drawings, tracings
    — Written words in addition to any of the above
— Materials are plentiful, support a wide range of play, and reflect children's family lives.
  — In the *sand and water area*
    — Fill-and-empty materials
    — Floating materials
    — Pretend-play materials
    — Alternatives to sand and water
    — Waterproof gear and tidy up materials
  — In the *block area*
    — Building materials
    — Take-apart-and-put-together materials
    — Fill-and-empty materials
    — Pretend-play materials
    — Reference photos
  — In the *house area*
    — Cooking and eating equipment
    — Pretending and role-play materials
    — Homelike materials reflecting children's family lives
    — Real cooking equipment (for use with adult supervision)
    — Reference photos and recipes
  — In the *art area*
    — Paper
    — Painting and printing materials
    — Fasteners
    — Modelling and moulding materials
    — Collage materials
    — Drawing and cutting materials
  — In the *toy area*
    — Sorting and small building materials
    — Take-apart-and-put-together materials
    — Pretend-play materials
    — Games

— In the *book and writing area*
  — Books
  — Magazines
  — Storytelling props
  — Writing materials
— In the *woodworking area*
  — Tools
  — Fasteners
  — Wood and building materials
— In the *music and movement area*
  — Percussion instruments
  — Simple wind instruments
  — Recording equipment, recorded music, and players
  — Props for dancing
— In the *computer area*
  — Computer(s) that are multimedia and up to date (with speakers if you wish to play music)
  — Software programs appropriate for young children
  — Printer(s) (preferably colour)
— In the *outdoor area*
  — Stationary structures
  — Wheeled toys
  — Loose materials

Taken from *Educating Young Children Third Edition*
By Mary Hohmann, David P. Weikart and Ann S. Epstein

Box 4.3 A visit to a preschool in a Victorian house

The ground floor of this Victorian house built in 1899 is the home base for twenty-four 3- and 4-year-olds and three practitioners. With many original features, such as an impressive staircase, fireplaces, doors and wooden floors, it makes a spacious and homely learning environment. The four original rooms have been modified to allow children to move freely between them while retaining a distinct feel to match the purpose of each interest area.

In the entrance hall each child has a space marked with their photo and name for hanging outdoor clothes. Above the coat hooks is information for parents and carers, displaying photographs of the daily routine with a brief written explanation of each segment, and on a whiteboard there is a photograph of each key worker with a list of their allocated children and a note of the activities planned for small group time and large group time. In contrast to the activity in this part of the hallway at arrival and departure times, at work time the corner where the wide staircase goes round creates a naturally cosy and comfortable *book area*, which is quiet and away from the bustle at work time. Two child-size easy chairs, a rug, large book stand, book rack and a basket of puppets bring a softness to this well-used and calm haven.

The front room is called the *carpet area* and is the largest area, with ample room for all the children and practitioners to gather for greeting time and large group time. During work time many children, and the practitioner assigned to the area, are lying, sitting and standing, building large block structures, making complex train lines and marble runs. The children select and put away the construction and small world materials they need from accessible, labelled storage along each side of the room. Three-year-old Charlie returns several times to play his favourite spider-man game in the dolls' house.

Joining the carpet area is the middle room, delineated by wooden flooring and rugs. This space houses a *home area*, spacious enough for a child-size bed and wicker chairs as well as kitchen amenities, dolls and buggies, the *writing area* and the *finding out area*. In the home area the children planned to make a roof using a sheet, which involved a degree of problem solving to make it stay in place, and detail including autumn leaves in the 'gutter'. At work time, 'dog play' and dancing around the kitchen table were highlights enjoyed by the children. The writing area has a round table alongside an open, wooden storage unit. There is a flurry of activity here at work time, with a full table of children and a practitioner, collecting, using and returning paper, scissors, glue, clipboards, magazines, felt-tip pens, crayons and pencils, as needed for their plans. The finding out area, with its magnifiers, magnets, fir cones, leaves, conkers and timers created a corner for a small group time activity with peg boards.

The back of the ground floor in this setting is on a slightly lower level and four steps and a banister lead from the writing area and finding out area to the lino-floored *sand area, water area, play dough area* and *art area* in the adjoining room. At work time today Charlie and his friend Bethan, both aged 3 years, spent over twenty minutes at a busy play dough table cutting up play dough to make dinner. They then went into the art area and used shaving foam to make marshmallows to barbeque, and then chose scourers, sponges and paint brushes to make lines and patterns in more shaving foam. At tidy-up time Bethan independently got a knife and scraped the play dough from her shoes and put it in the bin, returning the knife to the play dough storage unit. The children washed their hands at the low-level sink and used the paper towel dispenser, before snack time was served at the tables in the art area. After this they put their cartons in the bin and plates in the dish washer.

This setting serves 170 families with places for children aged 0–5 years and is housed in two identical Victorian houses, and the consistent lay-out of interest areas aids transition and familiarity for the children and visitors. The interest areas are labelled with large, clear area signs with the words and pictures denoting the activities that can be found there. The materials in each interest area are easily accessible, maintained and topped up as necessary and are labelled using pictures, photographs, outlines or the actual object, with the words included on some of the labels. There is an emphasis on literacy in the environment, with planning and recall cards in each interest area for each key group, as well as planning and recall cards on key rings to remind children of ideas for their plans and activities. These are attached to the wall using Velcro or hooks. Message boards for each of the three key person groups are left out for children to re-visit and there are a large whiteboard and chalk board for mark making on the wall in the writing area and art area. The daily routine chart, with photographs of each segment of the day, is prominent on the carpet area wall space, so children and visitors can identify what happens next. Large whiteboards with named magnets for each child help to organise the collection of on-going anecdotal observation notes before they are transferred to each child's 'learning journey' file. Display boards reflect small group time project work and children's art, and there is a large, low-level mirror in the carpet area. Each child has his own accessible storage space in the art area for keeping reminders of home, work to take home and treasured possessions.

Large windows to the front of the house are used as a waving space, and together with double patio doors onto the outside learning environment afford plenty of natural light. The children have 45 minutes' outdoor time towards the end of the session. The patio doors open onto a wooden decking space with a single step down to a cycle track around a central picnic table and chairs and climbing frame. In one corner there is a raised, covered platform like a pagoda and on the other side there are wooden tunnels, dens, slides and steps, with a sand table in the middle. Old-fashioned kitchen sinks are used as planters and there are raised beds with shrubs and flowers. The space is subtly zoned for physical, dramatic, social, imaginative and natural play, with spaces delineated by a variety of surfaces: brick paving, wooden decking, bark, artificial grass and fixed wooden structures. There are two sheds, one free standing and one under the fire escape, both with accessible, labelled storage.

Charlie starts his outdoor time by dropping balls onto gutter pipes and pipe junctions fixed to the brick wall. There is lots of giggling when practitioner Justyna shows the children how to juggle. Three-year-old Bethan wipes rain water off the table and chairs and soon a group of children gather round the table to chat. The cycle track has a traffic jam and a group of children by the pagoda turn into hopping bunnies. Bethan chooses to play hide and seek with plastic numbers in the sand tray with several other children and practitioner Angela. Charlie stands and looks up at the sky, noticing the unusual patterns made by the cloud formation and discusses this with Sue, the nursery manager. A sudden gust of wind shifts the plastic tunnel and everyone gasps.

The morning ends with large group time when the children return to the carpet area. Bethan lays out the small toys from the 'singing sack' and Charlie chooses to sing 'Pop goes the weasel'.

The outside learning environment

Young children like and need to be outdoors where they can make large movements and use loud voices in an unconstrained way. The need for fresh air, exercise and contact with nature is invigorating and can lead adults to learn about children's different abilities and interests.

In HighScope settings how the outdoor learning environment is used will depend on the nature of the premises and will be planned as either a discrete time period or open access during work time (Chapter 5). In any event, the children will go outside every day.

Just like the indoor space, the outdoor space has separate areas for physically vigorous play and areas for focused play, so children can, for example, dig in the soil without having to watch out for children riding wheeled toys or zooming off the slide. There are areas for digging, planting and observing insects and birds, areas to sit with friends and chat or just watch others play and an area for pretend play.

Outside play materials will include fixed structures for climbing, swinging and sliding; wheeled toys for pushing and pulling and loose materials like pine cones, small logs, hoops and balls for combining, transforming and transporting. The use of real, open-ended materials like tyres, crates, planks, pipes and sheets creates many opportunities for exploring, pretending and building for intentional, purposeful play. There is safe accessible storage for outdoor materials, for example, labelled parking bays for wheeled toys and labelled containers for loose materials which can be stored in a well-organised shed.

The role of outdoor play in the HighScope approach is the same as indoor play; to support children in their active learning adventures and thereby foster intrinsic motivation and the key developmental indicators. Adults and children share control and the practitioners help children to obtain the materials they need and use work time support strategies (Chapter 5). The outdoor learning environment has the additional benefits of fresh air, the freedoms of using larger movements, louder voices and appreciating the beauty and wonder of nature. In countries where the climate is suitable HighScope may have a completely outdoor classroom, with all parts of the daily routine outside.

Maintaining and developing the learning environment

Materials will be well used in an active learning setting and maintenance and development of the learning environment in HighScope settings is on-going. This includes a daily visual check that materials are clean, safe and well maintained, that broken items are removed and that the art area is well stocked with consumable items such as paper. Observation records help practitioners to support the key developmental indicators by identifying any gaps in relevant provision and additional materials or areas are added to match children's current interests. Labelling is replaced periodically and areas are observed to see when they may need refreshing in order to invite renewed interest and learning opportunities. An essential part of long-term planning is to maintain and develop the learning environment, with regular evaluation and audits (see 'curriculum assessment' in Chapter 7).

Key points

1. The learning environment is designed to meet the needs of children as active learners so that they feel safe, valued, adventurous and competent.
2. The HighScope approach can be used anywhere, using real, open-ended and commercial materials which reflect children's interests.
3. Interest areas are defined by the kinds of play children typically engage in – sensory exploration, building, creating things, pretending, using books and playing simple games – and have simple names the children understand.
4. While the storage of materials is consistent, the use of materials is flexible and children may take materials from one area to another, returning them at tidy-up time.
5. Adults do not limit the number of children who can use a given area at any time and use this as an opportunity to evaluate the interest areas, share control with children and solve problems over space and materials.
6. Storage empowers children to find, use and return materials on their own as they pursue their own plans and intentions.

7. Labelling goes from concrete to abstract and will include a variety of the following: the actual object, photograph, picture, line drawing, silhouette, photocopy, or any of these, along with the word.
8. Less is more, for example a single line of puzzles is easier for children to access than a stack of puzzles.
9. There will be designated space to display children's unfinished and finished 2D and 3D work.
10. Practitioners regularly use the key developmental indicators to audit materials and room arrangement.

Reflections on the HighScope approach

1. The environment and your philosophy
   - What is the relationship between the physical environment of your setting and your philosophy?
   - Does the environment help or hinder what you do?
   - What changes could you make?
2. The space is inviting to children and adults
   - How easy is it for new adults and children to find their way around your classroom?
   - How does your setting make you feel?
   - Is there an area you would like to revitalise? How will you do this?
3. Materials are plentiful and support a wide range of play experiences
   - What materials do your children find appealing?
   - How do they reflect children's family lives?
   - What do you have too much of?
   - What do you need to add to?
4. Display
   - How do you value children's 2D and 3D work so they view themselves as creative?
   - What do you do with unfinished work?
5. Indoors and outdoors
   - Do you make full use of learning opportunities outdoors in all weathers?
   - What materials do you have outside for children to combine, transform and transport?
   - Do your guidelines for indoor storage apply equally to outside storage?

Related reading

Epstein, A. (2007) *Essentials of Active Learning in Preschool – Getting to know the HighSope curriculum*. Ipsilanti, MI: HighScope Press

Goldschmied, E. and Jackson, S. (1994) *People Under Three – Young Children in Day Care*. London and New York: Routledge

Hohmann, M., Weikart, D. P. and Epstein, A. (2008) *Educating Young Children. The Complete Guide to the HighScope Preschool Curriculum* (3rd edn). Ipsilanti, MI: HighScope Press

Post, J., Hohmann, M., & Epstein, A. S. (2011). *Tender Care and Early Learning: Supporting Infants and Toddlers in Child Care Settings* (2nd edn). Ypsilanti, MI: HighScope Press

Theemes, T. (1999) *Let's Go Outside: Designing the Early Childhood Playground*. Ypsilanti, MI: HighScope Press

Vogel, N. (2009). *Setting Up the Preschool Classroom*. Ypsilanti, MI: HighScope Press

5 The daily routine

This chapter explains the use of time in a HighScope setting and the rationale behind it. It describes the components of a HighScope daily routine and what a typical day might look like. It then looks in more depth at how the daily routine provides a flexible framework for active learning and achieves a balance between child- and adult-initiated activities. HighScope's essential and unique element, plan-do-review, is discussed, as are the adult-initiated periods: greeting time, large group time and small group time. It considers outside time and transitions between the key components of the daily routine to ensure the day has balance, flow and momentum. Finally, it explains how children learn the daily routine and describes a morning in the lives of 2-year-old Henrik and 4-year-old Anna, who attend HighScope settings.

Introduction and rationale for a daily routine

It is important to understand that the HighScope approach daily routine is enabling rather than prescriptive and fully supportive of the ethos of active learning and shared control.

Having a consistent yet flexible routine is important for all of us. For an adult, this seems to come to light especially when a change occurs: from having visitors to starting university, having a baby or changing one's job. Adjustments have to be made and time allowed to settle into a new routine and to feel comfortable. For children, a predictable routine, when they know what will happen next, gives great security, especially during settling-in periods and for children who have English as an additional

Figure 5.1 The HighScope Wheel of Learning with the Daily Routine section highlighted

Source: Hohmann, Weikart and Epstein (2008, p. 6)

language. A consistent daily routine can provide a framework for teaching and learning. It frees children and adults from worrying about what comes next and it enables them to use their creative energies for the task at hand.

With so many psychological and educational benefits, HighScope has from the beginning paid significant attention to the detail of how to apply active learning to every moment of the day. In the HighScope curriculum, adults aim to share control with children throughout the day, and both the practitioners and children initiate activities. In practice, the interplay between the well-organised learning environment with materials accessible to children and a defined daily routine facilitates this. It is a subtle structure supporting the ethos behind active learning and shared control.

The HighScope daily routine is designed to accomplish several key goals. These are to provide children with:

- a consistent, predictable sequence of events that gives them a sense of control over what happens next and a stable and secure psychological environment within which they are free to make choices and initiate activities
- a plan-do-review experience
- different types of interactions, small and large groups, adult to child, child to child
- time for play and learning inside, outside and on outings
- time for both adult- and child-initiated activities.

In addition to these goals, there is an opportunity in the early years to role model a balanced daily routine so that children can draw on what this looks and feels like throughout their life.

HighScope preschool daily routine components

A typical HighScope day includes both adult-initiated and child-initiated periods, and is made up of:

greeting time (variable)
large group time (10–15 minutes)
small group time (15–20 minutes)
planning time (10–15 minutes)
work time (45–60 minutes)
tidy-up time (10 minutes)
recall time (10–15 minutes)
outside time (30–40 minutes)
transition times, including arrival and departure (variable)
eating and resting times (variable).

The order of components may vary, depending on the hours and structure of the setting. However, plan-do-review, which includes planning time, work time, tidy-up time and recall time always occur in that order. In half-day provision, each component typically happens once. In full-day provision, one or more components may be repeated.

It is a flexible framework and can take into account the schedules of childminders and parents, including visits to childminder 'drop in centres' and school pick-ups. Although the routine is the same each day, it can accommodate special events like outings or one-off visits. While they are flexible, the timings are seen as significant because they are roughly the amount of time for which children can concentrate. A large group time lasting 30 minutes will result in fidgety children, while work time lasting two hours will lose momentum. Because the routine and learning environment are consistent, children know they will be able to do the things they like again the next day.

Box 5.1 Sample daily routines

Half-Day Programme

⇨ Greeting time
⇨ Planning, work, tidy up, and recall time
⇨ Snack
⇨ Large-group time
⇨ Small-group time
⇨ Outside time
⇨ Departure

Morning arrival group:
⇨ Greeting time
⇨ Planning, work, tidy up, and recall time
⇨ Small-group time
⇨ Large-group time
⇨ Outdoor time
⇨ Lunch
⇨ Departure

Afternoon arrival group:
⇨ Lunch
⇨ Greeting time
⇨ Large-group time
⇨ Planning, work, tidy up, and recall time
⇨ Small-group time
⇨ Snack
⇨ Outdoor time
⇨ Departure

Full-Day Programme

⇨ Breakfast
⇨ Greeting time
⇨ Large-group time
⇨ Planning, work, tidy up, and recall time
⇨ Small-group time
⇨ Outside time
⇨ Lunch
⇨ Books and rest
⇨ Snack
⇨ Outside time
⇨ Departure

Staggered arrivals and departures through the day:
⇨ Free play
⇨ Breakfast
⇨ Greeting time
⇨ Planning, work, tidy up, and recall time
⇨ Small-group time
⇨ Large-group time
⇨ Outside time
⇨ Lunch
⇨ Books, nap
⇨ Snack
⇨ Small-group time
⇨ Planning, work, and tidy up, and recall time with parents

Taken from *Essentials of Active Learning in Preschool: Getting to Know the HighScope Curriculum* by Ann S. Epstein

Child-initiated periods of the HighScope daily routine

The key periods of the day for child-initiated activity are part of the plan-do-review cycle and consist of:

- planning time
- work time
- tidy-up time
- recall time.

The plan-do-review process is the essential centrepiece of the HighScope daily routine and enhances child-initiated periods to support the development of increasingly complex play.

The individual segments of plan-do-review, when taken together, provide the longest part of the day, lasting approximately 1½ hours. The fact that child-initiated rather than adult-initiated experiences constitute the majority of the day emphasises the importance of children taking control of and responsibility for their own learning. It balances the adult-initiated activities, while making it clear that children's own interests – and a consideration of their individual developmental and ability levels – should predominate in carrying out the curriculum.

Plan-do-review

Plan-do-review is strongly represented in the HighScope research, where there is hard evidence that its outcomes produce dispositions that are favourable in society (Schweinhart et al., 2005). The research shows that, in the short-term, plan-do-review gives children many opportunities for initiative, independence, problem solving and decision making, and when experienced systematically, this leads to the long-term benefits of positive attitudes to learning and social responsibility in adulthood. It is believed to be very empowering for a child to develop a sense of competency and control, and that knowing that adults value your actions is a significant factor in the development of positive self-esteem. This is why plan-do-review has a high status in the daily routine, particularly, for children who are disadvantaged.

Planning time

HighScope practitioners value planning in all its forms and respond equally to vague, routine and elaborate planners (Berry and Sylva, 1987). In order to plan, children must be able to hold in mind a picture of something that is not actually present or that has not yet happened. For babies and toddlers who are not at that developmental stage, plan-do-review is known as choice time. Planning, doing and reviewing are combined and adults will begin this developmental process by modelling the language, for example: "You have decided to play in the sand" (planning) and "I saw you filling your bucket" (review). Planning as a discrete time will begin in the late toddler or preschool years.

Figure 5.2 Planning time (photo: M. Wiltshire)

Planning time takes about 10–15 minutes and begins the plan-do-review sequence. Planning is intended to help children to develop specific ideas about what they want to do and how they will do it. This means that when children start to play it will involve more purpose and intentionality than just choosing what to do because children will have thought about what they want to do before they do it. Planning will look different for children at different stages of development, beginning with children expressing their plans in actions (picking up a paint brush) and gestures (pointing to the art area) and progressing to words ("I'm going to make a painting of my house"). With first-hand experience, practice and familiarity with materials, children's planning drawings will develop from marks and scribbles to include shapes, simple figures and objects, through to more detailed, distinct figures. In the planning drawing in Figure 5.3, Claire had recently seen model dinosaurs at a museum.

Figure 5.3 Planning drawing: by Claire aged 4 years "I am going to make a paper model dinosaur and play cars."

Planning strategies

Practitioners look at ways to make planning easy for children and ensure that it takes place in an intimate setting in the same small, stable group as recall and small group time. Strategies to match children's developmental levels and interests are used to engage children in what is a brief, playful and varied occasion. Ideas for planning time will vary from concrete to abstract. This means that you could see the practitioner reminding children of what they might like to do by uncovering a tray with a paint brush, block, book and doll on it and asking children to make a choice. Similarly, the practitioner might use picture cards representing materials from the different areas of the setting or help the children to link together in a train that goes from one interest area to another, allowing children to make a plan when they arrive at an area where they want to play. Props like telephones or puppets can be used to initiate planning, or making rhymes with children's names to indicate who plans next. Drawing pictures of materials, actions, people and other things involved in the plan; taking dictation from children or having children write down letters and words in their plan are increasingly abstract ways of planning with children. There are as many ideas for planning as the practitioners' and children's imaginations will allow.

Whatever the strategy, the aim is that every child is able to understand and perform it in some way, consistent with his developmental abilities. Planning strategies are never used as a 'test' of children's knowledge and practitioners are sensitive to any worries or concerns which may impede a child's planning, such as the loss of a favourite pet or that a special friend he wants to play with hasn't arrived yet. When child–adult ratios are too high for creating an intimate, cosy group, the practitioner might plan with half the group on alternate sessions, make use of peer planning or use parent volunteers to ensure that enough attention is given to every child.

The ethos of planning

Children will sometimes change their plans as they carry out their ideas or become interested in what someone else is doing. Therefore, in HighScope settings children are not required to stick to their initial plan or criticised for not completing it. Instead, adults follow up with children at work time and help them to express a new plan. Children may also complete their initial plan and then, often with the practitioner's encouragement, come up with another plan to continue their work time activity. It is not necessary to express a plan before every change of activity, but it is the general ethos behind planning as a developmental process that is important.

In summary, the purpose of planning time is to:

- encourage children to articulate their ideas, choices and decisions
- promote children's self-confidence and sense of control
- lead to involvement and concentration on play
- support the development of increasingly complex play.

Work time

Work time is the 'do' part of the plan-do-review sequence. It lasts for 45 minutes to an hour and is a busy part of the day. It is both purposeful and playful, as children have thought about their plans, which may span from two minutes to fifteen minutes to the whole of work time. Some

Figure 5.4 Work time (photo: M. Wiltshire)

plans may also spread over several consecutive work times and become more of a large-scale project. During work time children have an uninterrupted period of time to work on activities of their own choosing. HighScope believes that children learn through play, and calling this segment 'work time' captures this philosophy. Work time promotes children's innate desire and need to explore, experiment, invent, construct and pretend, in short, to play. Activities are diverse and might include, for example, making hands by filling rubber gloves with water, making secret models called 'senna' from clay and sticks, dressing up and making up a line dance on the stage in the block area or carrying out a long-term project of wrapping tape round a table.

Practitioners are available throughout this time as participant observers to guide and scaffold learning. HighScope has clearly defined the adult role during this core period and practitioners will use the following proactive strategies.

- *They provide interest areas and materials based on children's interests*
  Work time could not happen without a thoughtful, well-organised learning environment, as this will enable the opportunities for independence, decision making, initiative and problem solving. In order to create and carry out plans children are given appealing, open-ended materials which they can access easily.

- *They offer children comfort and contact as needed*
  Practitioners watch out for any signs of children needing this most basic kind of emotional support. Children may be frustrated, out of sorts, anxious, unsure or stressed by events over which they have no control and may express this by pouting, withdrawing to a corner, or calling out incessantly. Practitioners provide whatever acknowledgement or reassurance they know that child will need, be it a smile, a hug or looking at something a child has done.

- *They participate in children's play*
  Practitioners are available and involved in children's play and pay particular attention to joining in respectfully without disrupting the children's flow and joining only when it suits the children's plan and situation, thereby allowing the children to retain control. They do this by initially looking around the play space to silently observe and listen, so as to help them understand the role children might want them to take. By playing alongside and as partners with children, practitioners

can and often do extend the length and scope of some play episodes. Beyond this, they may challenge in a gentle way young children's thinking and reasoning to expand the breadth of their play and, consequently, their understanding. However, this is all within the context of the on-going play.

■ *They converse with children*
Encouraging children to use language is one of the ingredients of active learning which will help them to internalise new knowledge. Practitioners look for natural opportunities for conversation without interrupting children's flow and indicate a genuine partnership approach by using their natural voice, having balanced conversations and limiting questions. Child-initiated play is seen as an ideal time to introduce 'rare' words in a meaningful context to build vocabulary and develop other language skills that are important in early literacy development. (See Chapter 6 for more on these strategies.)

■ *They encourage children's problem solving*
In an environment that fosters active learning there will be both physical problems – "I can't find the end of the tape" – and social problems – "She took my truck" – to solve. Recognising the enormous learning value in these situations, practitioners will see supporting the process, as opposed to being responsible for finding solutions, as a key part of their role. It is common to hear practitioners say things like "I can see you have a problem", "I know you are upset", "What could you do to sort this out?" "Would you like my help?" (see Chapter 6). Practitioners find that supporting the process of problem solving rather than taking responsibility for finding the solutions helps them to take a calm approach when conflicts and issues arise, and leads to children becoming competent problem solvers themselves. Practitioners also often refer one child to another, which empowers the child who assists and enables the problem solver to view peers as resources to draw on.

■ *They observe and record what children do*
There will be many learning moments at work time which practitioners capture in a brief anecdote of what a child has done or said that is significant to their development. Practitioners keep pen and paper to hand and devise abbreviations to keep this process simple. There is no defined number of observations to collect: on some days each practitioner may record three observations, on other days more. These

recorded observations provide evidence of what is happening in the classroom, and are used to plan for the next day (see Chapter 7).

■ *They bring work time to an end with tidy-up time*
Tidy-up time brings work time to a close and will be done by both adults and children. Practitioners will have noted a tidy-up time strategy on their daily planning sheet beforehand. For example, this could be a tidy-up time song to a familiar tune, 'If you're happy and you know it, find a toy', or asking children to pick out an interest-area

Figure 5.5 Tidy-up time (photo: M. Wiltshire)

card or 'ticket' from a basket and tidy up in that area. Practitioners will let children know a short while beforehand that tidy-up is about to happen and then work with the children to clean up and put materials away. The well-organised learning environment plays a large part in adults and children being able to share this task and there are cloths and child-size brooms available. With realistic expectations, the learning environment will be restored to order in 10–15 minutes, though sometimes practitioners will call a halt to the process and acknowledge, "We've worked hard on this" and move on to recall time.

In summary, work time is intended to:

- help children to carry out intentions and to play with purpose
- enable children to participate in a social setting
- provide many opportunities to solve problems
- enable children to construct their own knowledge as they engage in the key developmental indicators
- allow adults to observe, learn from and support children's play.

Recall time

Older toddlers and preschoolers have a designated recall time lasting for 10–15 minutes and this completes the plan-do-review process. Recall, also known as review time, is when children tell or show each other something they did at work time. There is great personal interest in telling someone about something you have done, and recall time promotes natural speaking, listening and thinking opportunities for children in the company of attentive and interested adults and peers. Children tell their stories in their own words and take time to think about not only what they did but also what they learned. Which part of work time they choose to recall, or their perceptions, may be surprising. For example:

Child: "I played hide and seek on my own"
Adult: "What was that like?"
Child: "I played with my invisible dog"

Recall is seen as a developmental process supported by the practitioner who was present at work time so that they can have genuine conver-

Figure 5.6 Recall time (photo: M. Wiltshire)

sations, and also remind children who have fewer verbal skills what they saw them doing. While the recall process generally involves discussions, young children will also use motions and gestures, re-enactments, drawings and written accounts to describe their work time experiences. Even with more verbally able children, recall conversations will include conversational strategies such as contributing, commenting, repeating, acknowledging and using questions thoughtfully and sparingly.

Recall strategies

Practitioners support recall in the same way as planning, meeting with the same familiar group of children in a consistent place to create a comfortable and trusting situation. As with planning, props and games keep recall interesting and help children to wait for their turn. For example, the children might be invited to make a 'tour' of the room to the areas where they have played, each child bringing an item he or she played with to the recall table. Alternatively, photographs taken at work time might be used to spark conversations about what children did. The

Figure 5.7 Recall drawing: by Adewel aged 4 years "I played snap."

materials or activity are kept simple so that they do not become an activity in themselves and the purpose of recall is not lost.

The ethos of recall

With the understanding that children's capacity to recall develops over time and with experience, practitioners can support all sorts of recall that make sense to each child. Children are comfortable participating in recall experiences in a way that is playful, gives them control over the stories they will tell and encourages them to contribute to one another's narratives. Where child–adult ratios are high, adults may be able to take more of an unhurried and relaxed approach by recalling with half the children in each recall group each day, or by using parent volunteers.

As children grow in their ability to articulate what they want to do and construct memories in words, their understanding of the connections between their plans and recall narratives becomes increasingly apparent.

In summary, the purpose of recall time is to:

- exercise children's capacities to form and talk about mental images
- consolidate children's understanding of experiences and events
- extend children's consciousness beyond the present
- make children's experiences public.

Adult-initiated periods of the HighScope daily routine

The key periods of the day for adult-initiated activity are:

- greeting time
- large group time
- small group time

Greeting time

Greeting time is a small but crucial part of the daily routine which gets the day off to a good start and creates a comfortable atmosphere for learning. There are two adults in flexible roles, one to greet parents and one to support the children. This ensures that everyone is warmly greeted and listened to at what can otherwise be a demanding time during the transition from home to school. Preferably, children meet in an area close to the entrance so that they are not passing materials which will not be available until work time. They have access to a small range of materials, enabling them to make a choice and stay active, supported by an adult, until the start of the message board. Most often, children look at books during this time. Parents are welcomed to stay as long as they can and look at books together with the children.

The message board

The message board immediately follows greeting time and is when children and practitioners talk through what is going to happen. Since children do not always arrive at the exact same time, practitioners generally wait until everyone is there before children put away the books or other quiet materials they were looking at during the arrival period and move to the message board so everyone can learn about the day's events together. Together they 'read' three or four messages about the day's events which have been prepared ahead of time on a whiteboard or

Figure 5.8 Greeting time (photo: M. Wiltshire)

on chart paper. The messages are written using a combination of pictures, letters and words so that children at different levels of literacy and facility with language can 'read' them. They typically concern absences, visitors, changes to the routine, new materials or any news; and messages that relate to the children's daily lives and to experiences that are important to them. Each setting will use common symbols for interest areas – as well as their written words – and parts of the daily routine, along with universally known symbols such as the 'no' symbol of a circle crossed with a diagonal line. Practitioners and regular visitors may have their photograph or a symbol representing distinctive characteristics. For example, a visitor who has come to observe may be drawn as a stick person holding paper and pencil, so that children know they will not be playing with them. As well as simple drawings and photographs, actual objects can be taped to the board, for example, a CD indicating that there will be music and movement at large group time. Simple and familiar words or numbers, such as 'Art Area' or 'Blocks' or '2' help children begin to acquire literacy knowledge. Parents sometimes join this period of the day if their schedules permit. When children are developmentally

Figure 5.9 Message board (photo: M. Wiltshire)

ready, they will contribute to this session with some of the most meaningful messages *to* children generated *by* children.

The message board is the HighScope alternative to calendar time,
weather board, 'letter of the week' and other traditional greeting activities. HighScope practitioners believe it offers rich reading, writing,
numeracy and group problem-solving opportunities in a meaningful
context, as well as engendering a sense of self-esteem and well-being at
the start of the day.

Large group time

Large group time, sometimes known as circle time, is there to give a
sense of community and is a time for songs, stories, re-enacting and cooperative games. Specifically, in HighScope it involves all adults and all
children and will last around 10–15 minutes. Each day practitioners will

Figure 5.10 Large group time (photo: M. Wiltshire)

discuss ideas taken from children's interests, curriculum content in physical development and the arts (KDIs), co-operative play or projects and events that are currently meaningful to the children to make plans for large group time. Whilst this is an adult-initiated part of the day, the distinction between adult 'initiated' and adult 'directed' is made and practitioners will keep the ingredients of active learning in mind, bringing in opportunities for action, choice and interests both in the planning and in flexibility during the activity. In a HighScope large group time, it is common for children to say, "I've got an idea!" and then assume a leadership role to change a song, introduce a movement, add to a story or modify a game. Practitioners will have a repertoire of songs and games to serve as starting-points to which children can bring new variations if wanted. Song cards or hand-made class song books with symbols and words are used to give children choice and help them to remember both old favourites and new songs. This is intended to balance the practitioner's need for control and children's need for action.

For example, in a typical large group time session the songs and games will be chosen, practised and materials prepared. Practitioners start straight away, with the first children gathered, with a simple repetitive activity, for example singing 'Everybody do this, do this, do this, everybody do this just like Catherine'. Catherine then points to Jodie, who chooses an action, and so on. They will then briefly introduce the next experience, for example re-enacting a nursery rhyme using simple props, and join in at the children's level. Having introduced the main activity they watch and listen to the children and follow up on their suggestions and ideas, giving them an opportunity to be the leaders. The final large group experience will include putting the materials away and will be linked as a transition to the next part of the daily routine, for example, by children marching to their small group time table.

Small group time

As the name implies, small group time is when a group of 8–10 children meet with an adult to experience active learning in a close and familiar setting. The group size will vary, depending on the adult–child ratios, but if it becomes too large it is likely that the practitioner will have two

Figure 5.11 Small group time (photo: M. Wiltshire)

groups and alternate between interacting with and overseeing them or use parent volunteers. The same group of children will meet together each day for 15–20 minutes with the same adult. This is the same grouping that meets for planning and recall time, and this arrangement will last for several months at a time.

The reason for these stable groups is to help practitioners to get to know each child and to help children feel comfortable with one another. For babies and young toddlers, practitioners will prepare small group time but this will be more fluid and dynamic, developing into a separate time period only when the children are ready. As at large group time, the same distinction is made between 'adult-initiated' activities and 'adult-directed' activities, and children will be given their own materials, will make choices about how to use them and will talk with one another and the adult about what they are doing, thus keeping the ingredients of active learning in mind.

In this intimate setting children who play by themselves at work time will play next to other children at small group time, be introduced to materials and experiences they might otherwise miss and have new ideas to incorporate into play at work time. Adults have a daily opportunity to observe and match their interaction strategies to the varying developmental levels and range of responses within their group. They will then be supporting children's current levels of development to consolidate learning and offering gentle extensions when children are ready.

Planning for small group time

As with large group time, practitioners plan daily, using either children's interests, curriculum content, new, unexplored, under-used or favourite materials, local traditions or community events. This gives a wealth of ideas to make sure the session engages children in an individualised learning experience. The following description of small group time summarises what is important and what is different in the HighScope approach, taking the experience from being simply an activity to active learning.

Practitioners prepare materials for each child beforehand, using either individual containers or shared materials, and have some 'back up' materials ready to extend children's interest in the activity if necessary. They begin by making a brief introductory statement or story, like, "One day some bears set out on a boat, I wonder where they went. . .", and handing out materials straight away. As children explore the materials the practitioners move to their physical level, watch what children do with the materials and listen to what they say. Practitioners will be careful to notice what each child is doing by moving from child to child, making descriptive comments and talking with them, following their leads. They look for opportunities to refer one child to another for ideas and help. By knowing their group very well they will be able to scaffold each child's learning from the exploratory stage to more detailed stages of learning and development. When bringing small group time to a close, practitioners will give a time warning, "In five minutes we need to put our materials away", and let the children know that the materials used will be available at work time if they want to carry on using them. Tidying up is done by the adult and children together and is a defined part of small group time.

A difference between HighScope and traditional nursery practice is that small group time is a discrete time period, it is not part of 'free play' or 'continuous provision'. Children are not pulled out of free play or work time to take part in small group activities. Their child-initiated free play remains uninterrupted, and distinct from, the adult-initiated small group time. HighScope practitioners believe this has several benefits:

■ it is a focused time, with practitioners working with their key group of children (small group time occurs with the same group of children and the same adult)
■ there will be several small groups running consecutively, each planned with the children's needs, interests and abilities in mind
■ if adult- and child-initiated play happen at the same time, the adult supporting an adult-initiated activity is not available to fully support child-initiated play
■ it avoids children feeling obliged to carry out 'the practitioner's activity', which may be perceived as more important than their own.

Outside time

In HighScope settings there will be a discrete outside time lasting for 30–40 minutes. Small group time and large group time may also be held outdoors, but again, each is a distinct period during the day. Outside time is often scheduled at the beginning or end of the session to limit the number of transitions and the putting on or taking off of outdoor clothing. The principles relating to interest areas, to storage and materials in the learning environment and to adult–child interaction strategies at work time all apply equally at outside time. The only difference is the additional

Figure 5.12 Outside time (photo: M. Wiltshire)

benefits of fresh air, possibilities for larger and more vigorous movements, different pretend props and observing nature. The whole of the daily routine may occur out of doors where the climate allows.

Outdoor learning environments vary from setting to setting and High-Scope practitioners give much thought and planning to best use the available space. Typically, there will be some fixed structures and practitioners will add loose materials, both commercial and free and found, which children can combine, transform and transport. Practitioners also maximise the potential for planting, growing and for observing insects and wildlife.

Outside time presents many opportunities for learning, not only in the area of physical development, but in all the other domains of development as well. There are signs to read, leaves and rocks to arrange by colour or size, insects and clouds to study and social conflicts to resolve about who has the next turn on the slide. During this time HighScope practitioners participate as partners, talk to children and encourage them to solve problems.

Snack time

Snack time (or meals in a full-day setting) are also a discrete time period. (In some settings, where children arrive at different times, breakfast may be set out in a café-style arrangement.) Adults and children always eat together, typically in the same small groups they use for planning, recall and small group time. The primary purpose of snack times in the High-Scope approach is to provide children with nutritious food and to create a relaxed atmosphere for conversation and a shared (social) experience. HighScope practitioners also value other learning opportunities that arise naturally at snack time. For example, exploring the properties of the food using all their senses, which develops children's observational skills and scientific knowledge; taking turns setting out napkins, plates and eating utensils, which establishes one-to-one correspondence (a mathematics concept) and allows children to participate in the community of the group. It is also common for children to be involved in preparing fruit or savoury snacks, which again adds to their cognitive and social knowledge and skills.

Figure 5.13 Snack time (photo: M. Wiltshire)

Transitions

The term 'transitions' relates to the times in between the components of the daily routine, which in HighScope are treated as activities in themselves. The purpose of transitions is to give a steady flow and momentum to the day and avoid a lot of waiting time.

To enable smooth transitions and a calm start to the next part of the day, practitioners reduce the number of transitions until there are as few as possible; for example, having small group time follow recall time so that the grouping and location remain the same. Children are always given a time warning just before the transition, for example, "In five minutes it will be tidy-up time", and brief music and movement activities like "Which animal can we move like as we walk to the cloakroom?" are used to capture children's attention. One activity will start as soon as another finishes, and whenever possible children are offered choices during a transition: "You can stay at the table with us as we finish small group time, or you can go to the book area and look at some books."

Organisational structures also make a big difference to transitions and the smooth running of the day. In particular, in full-day care settings with staff on shifts there can be many transitions involving a change of people. One way HighScope practitioners address this is to have a breakfast club and afternoon club with separate staff so that children have their classroom staff for the core period of the day. Alternatively, they might employ separate rest time staff, again so that there is a full complement of staff for the core day. This kind of organisation helps to allow for daily team planning (see Chapter 7), which in turn helps the day to run smoothly.

Familiarity with the routine helps children to make transitions independently, and with a consistent learning environment and a consistent daily routine the children soon realise that there will be time to continue their play tomorrow.

How children learn the daily routine

The key practical strategy to help children learn the daily routine is the daily routine chart. This is a hallmark of a HighScope classroom and there will be a visual timetable displayed at the children's eye level. It can take many forms, using either photographs, pictures or simple line drawings that illustrate that segment of the routine, alongside the name

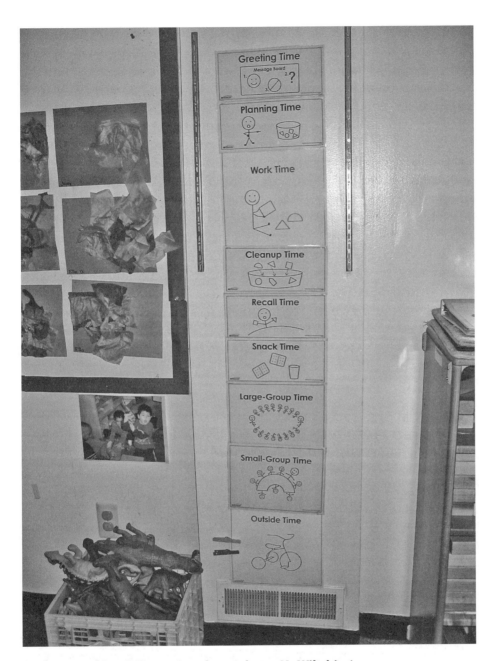

Figure 5.14 The daily routine chart (photo: M. Wiltshire)

of that part of the routine. It can be displayed vertically, horizontally or in a circle, with the size of each segment representing how long each part of the routine takes. The daily routine chart is frequently referred to, especially at the beginning of term or for new children.

For younger children or children with a short attention span, the concept is made more immediate by using a small, laminated picture of each part of the daily routine, placed on a ring which is then clipped onto the practitioner's clothing, for example a belt. This saves having to walk over to the daily routine chart on the wall.

For preschool children, strategies like children moving a Velcro mouse or clipping a peg to the appropriate segment are used to help them understand the order of the day. Changes to the routine are shown by using a blank card to cover a part of the chart. For example, the outside time card is covered when a visit to the pet shop is planned during outside time. It is in this personally meaningful way that children begin to understand the abstract concept of time. Public display of the daily schedule gives preschool children a concrete ownership of their day, giving them a sense of continuity, independence and control. Parents and visitors can also see the day at a glance.

The daily routine chart, along with consistency and a common language for components of the daily routine, enables children to become familiar with the sequence of events, and in turn to support new children and adults by explaining what comes next.

Box 5.2 A morning with Henrik (9.00–11.40), a 2-year-old in preschool

Henrik, aged 2 years and 4 months, is one of 13 children aged between 1 and 3 years in a toddler group called 'Bunnies' in a HighScope setting. He has been in this group since he was 1 year old. The setting is an English-speaking international preschool in Gothenburg, Sweden. Henrik's parents both speak Swedish at home and Henrik is bilingual. He started speaking English at preschool four months ago.

Greeting time (9.00)

As the two practitioners, Elisa and Sofia, sing "Who can find your pictures, your pictures, your pictures; the Bunnies can do that", to a familiar tune, Henrik sits on his 'spot', which is a photograph of himself and a picture of his favourite animal fixed to the floor with contact film. Henrik points to his friend's 'spot' and soon all the children and adults are sitting in a circle in the building area singing a welcome song called 'Choo, choo train'.

Elisa carries on greeting time using a message board. This is a whiteboard with four messages using photographs and pictures, each message being separated by a line. These indicate today's welcome song, who is here, what they will be doing for large group time and what is for snack. For example in the 'Who is here?' section, there are photographs of the practitioners who are in that day and photographs of the children who are absent; these are placed by either a picture of a house to indicate who is at home, a picture of a bed to indicate who is sick or a picture of an aeroplane to indicate who has gone abroad – a frequent occurrence in this international preschool. When Elisa says that Riku is at home today because his Mummy has a headache, Henrik says "Maybe she has bumped her head".

Large group time

Greeting time merges into large group time when Elisa points to the picture of the song bag on the message board and then holds up the bag itself. The song bag contains pictorial song cards which today have each been wrapped to add another element of surprise. In this activity the children take it in turns to pick a song card and then they all sing that song. Henrik says "sing" and "open" and points to Tom, the class persona doll who is sitting on the window sill. Tom joins the children and one by one they unwrap a song card covered in tissue paper. Henrik's card is 'Old MacDonald had a farm' and for this song each child is given an animal to hold. Jakob, sitting next to Henrik, holds a dog and calls out "Booster", which is the name of another child's dog that they see outside the preschool each morning. They pat a steady beat on their legs to the ABC song, sing the sleeping bunnie song and then give Tom, the persona doll, a hug goodbye.

Snack time

Still sitting in the large circle, the children have snack time. Henrik is today's 'special helper' and he hands out the snack boxes and water bottles. Henrik has a pear and spends some time peeling off a little bit of skin at a time and puts each piece in the bin. Seeing this, his practitioner, Elisa, peels it for him and he eats it all up. He takes a wet flannel from the bowl and wipes his face and hands.

Planning time (9.30)

Elisa has prepared a tray with an object from each interest area for planning time. There are a book, a doll, a Lego piece, a train track piece, a crayon and an empty shower gel bottle. As the children finish their snack each chooses an item and Elisa confirms that this is what they would like to do first at choice time.

Henrik picks up a crayon and Elisa says "You have chosen to draw in the art area Henrik."

Choice time

Henrik starts choice time drawing in the art area. He takes his paper and crayon from the accessible storage unit and after drawing brings the peg basket to the table and spends 15 minutes clipping the pegs round the edge of his paper. Next he gets a wooden shopping trolley and fills it with several home-made shaker bottles and pushes it back and forth between Bunnies room and the adjoining Pandas, room as the connecting door has been opened to increase the space and opportunities for choice time activities. For the next 35 minutes of choice time he does more 'shopping', fills toy trucks with brio trains and pushes them around. He spends a long time handing round colourful scarves from the home area to other children, who all put them on their own and the practitioners', heads. He then puts the scarf container right over his head and lifts it up and down saying "peep po", and he and the practitioners laugh. Three consecutive times he gets a tissue, wipes his nose and puts it in the bin. When a child is standing on the sofa he hears Elisa say, "We sit on the sofa, it's not safe to stand."

Elisa gives the children a warning that it is nearly tidy-up time and in five minutes they start to sing, "time to put the toys away, toys away, toys away" to the tune of London Bridge is falling down. After putting the Lego back in the box in the building area and the scarves back in the home area, Henrik sits on his 'spot'. He fastens the Velcro on his shoe and the practitioner says "Do you need my help?" to which he replies "No".

Recall time

The children divide into two groups for recall time. Elisa asks Henrik "What did you do at choice time?" and Henrik clearly replies "ABC". Following his lead, they all start to sing the ABC song and pat a steady beat on their legs. Knowing that Henrik can usually say something he has done, Elisa reminds him, saying "I saw you drawing", and Henrik says "Yes, pegs".

Small group time (10.30)

Still in the same group, which includes the four oldest children, Elisa asks the children to "Sit down and close your eyes". She brings out a dolls' house and a basket of people, and a farm and a basket of animals for small group time. This lasts for 15 minutes. Henrik plays with the play people, saying "Grandma, Papa, home", and Elisa says, "They can talk to each other, hello, how are you today?" Other small group times taking place at the same time include tearing, crumpling and 'reading' newspaper, and cutting and sticking.

Figure 5.15 Henrik at small group time (photo: M. Wiltshire)

Story time (10.50)

Next it is story time, and the children all sit on the sofa in the book area while Elisa reads 'Blue Hat, Green Hat' by Sandra Bounton. Henrik has his arm round Jakob and when the story characters go swimming he says in Swedish "I like to go swimming".

Lunch time (11.00)

The Bunnies children join the Pandas children for lunch time in their shared kitchen area. With five children seated at his table, Henrik eats sausages, potato and salad and has milk to drink. Several times he says "More please" and helps himself to more from small bowls at the table. When he has finished he gets down from the table, scrapes his plate in the bin and puts it in the sink. At the hand basin Elisa calls to him, "Have you got soap? Wash your hands then". After going to the toilet he gets his blanket and pillow from his drawer in the corridor and goes to lie down on his mattress in the Bunnies room, where the blinds have been drawn and there is gentle music playing.

In the afternoon he will have an hour's outside play.

Box 5.3 A morning with Anna (9.00 – 12.00), a 4-year-old in preschool

Anna is one of twenty 3- and 4-year-old children in the preschool group of a HighScope setting.

Greeting time (9.00)

Her morning begins with greeting time in the carpet area. All the children and all the practitioners gather together to sing some songs and one of the practitioners is playing a guitar. A child chooses a toy duck from the 'singing sack' and they all sing 'Three little ducks went swimming one day'. Then they sing their welcome song to the tune of Frère Jacques:

> We're at nursery, we're at nursery
> You are too, you are too
> We're pleased to see you, we're pleased to see you
> Lots to do, lots to do.

Next Anna and six other children go with their key worker, Sofka, for the message board session. Sofka has prepared three messages using words and symbols, and together they discuss that they will be having bananas and apples for snack time, how windy it is today and that there are four adults with them this morning, one of whom is a visitor who will be taking some photographs.

Small group time (9.20)

Already in the right location around the water tray for small group time, Sofka introduces the activity she has planned using shredded paper in the water tray and small world jungle animals. With back-up materials of grass and trees, play develops into talking about animals' homes, friendships and food and exploring the sounds they make. There are two other small group activities going on in the room; one exploring materials in the home area and one re-enacting the story of 'The Three Little Pigs' using puppets.

Planning time (9.40)

With the jungle animals back in the box in the carpet area (a large space for block and small world play), Sofka begins planning time with the same group of children using a planning card with photographs of the interest areas, and discusses what the children would like to do at work time. Anna points to the photograph of the home area and says that first she'll join the party her friends are planning. Then she points to the writing area. "What will you do in the writing area?" Sofka asks her. Anna replies, "Write my name". "Ah", says Sofka, "like you did yesterday at work time?" "Yes", says Anna, "with the clipboard." Sofka says, "I'll come by and see how you are getting on."

Work time (9.50)

Anna begins her work time dancing to music in the home area, led by a child holding a pink bag that plays music. She then goes to the writing area, takes a whiteboard and felt-tip pen from the storage unit and joins the other children sitting round the table. Next, she wipes her board, puts it away and gets an A5 clip board, an A4 sheet of paper and scissors. She places the clipboard over the paper and carefully cuts around the paper so it fits the clipboard. She finishes this off by pressing down on the clip board with one hand and tearing the last side of paper with the other hand. She clips her paper onto the clipboard and writes her name at the top of the paper. Then she asks Sofka to write her name, then on to Rosie, then to Jasper, and she continues going to several more children until the page is full of names, saying, "Can you write your name on my list?" "Very good", and "I need to do lots and lots and lots of names". Her

Figure 5.16 Anna at work time (photo: M. Wiltshire)

friends Rosie, Jasper and Harriet then start to do the same, getting their clipboards, paper and felt pens and go off collecting names. This activity lasts for 35 minutes. Anna then draws a picture which she describes to Sofka as "A house with no one in, as they have gone for a walk" and explains that "The princess is sad because she lives on her own". A friend asks Anna if she would like to do a 'twirly whirl' to music. Anna replies "No thanks" and goes to sit in the lap of another practitioner, called Lucy, in the home area. Her last work time activity is reading a book in the book area and, after a child with a sand timer tells her it is five minutes to tidy-up time, she goes to help Lucy and other children tidy up in the home area.

Recall time (10.50)

Sitting at a table in the art area Sofka uses the planning board with photos of the interest areas to talk about her key children's work time activities at recall time. Anna brings her list of names to show the recall group and reads them out.

Snack time (11.00)

The children then have apples and bananas and milk or water, which have been prepared by some children during work time. The main topic of conversation between the children at the snack table is about their visits to schools. When she finishes her snack, Anna puts her milk carton in the bin and her plate in the dish washer, and goes to put on her coat, hat and wellington boots for outside time.

Outside time (11.10)

Outside, Anna dances round and round a fixed wooden structure. She then goes into the 'wicker house', and with a friend makes 'fire' using two sticks, for the dinosaur to keep warm. Coming out of the house she pauses to watch a practitioner supporting conflict resolution with two children who both want the same tricycle. She finds a car for herself and drives around the cycle track. After 40 minutes outside Anna comes inside, takes off her wellington boots, coat and hat and sits in a large circle on the carpet area for large group time.

Large group time (11.45)

With a practitioner playing the guitar, each child is invited to choose an instrument. Anna chooses a bell, and when asked to choose a song for all the children to sing and play their instruments to, she chooses 'London Bridge is falling down'.

Anna's morning in preschool finishes when practitioner Sam says, "If your name begins with 'A' go and wash your hands for lunch".

Key points

1. The HighScope daily routine is a consistent yet flexible framework for active learning.
2. The framework is very adaptable and can be adjusted to suit different settings, different age groups and children of different abilities.
3. The main elements of the core day are plan-do-review (child initiated), greeting time, message board, large group time, small group time (adult initiated), outside time and snack time. Child choice and initiation predominate throughout the day, even during activities that are initiated by adults.
4. Some of the components of the daily routine can be moved around so that they happen in a different order, although plan-do-review is always consecutive and comprises the longest segment of the day.
5. Small group time for older toddlers and preschoolers is a separate time period and not within 'free play' or 'work time' as in traditional nursery practice.
6. Stable groups with the same adult and the same children at small group time, planning time and recall time support close personal relationships.
7. The daily routine chart and the message board (following greeting time) are practical strategies to support shared control between children and adults.
8. HighScope practitioners support children's progression within activities by expecting different levels of development and responses, and matching their interaction strategies accordingly.
9. This predictable routine, when children know what will happen next, gives great security, especially during settling-in periods and for children who have English as an additional language.
10. The HighScope daily routine gives children freedom and independence within a structured day, and with adult support and guidance they can develop their initiative and pursue their interests.

Reflections on the HighScope approach

1. Rhythm of the day:
   - How is the pattern of the day determined in your setting?
   - What are the fixed points in the day?

- What is the balance between adult and child-initiated play?
- How can you give children ownership of the daily routine?

2. Plan-do-review
   - What is your role during child-initiated play?
   - How do you use plan-do-review in your adult life?
   - What relevance does this have to plan-do-review as the centrepiece of the HighScope daily routine?

3. Large group time or circle time
   - How do you balance the children's need for action and the adult's need for control at large group time?
   - Which aspects of a HighScope large group time are familiar to you?
   - Are there any strategies you would like to add to large group time in your setting?

4. Small group time
   - What organisational strategies do you have for adult-initiated activities?
   - What do you think is the difference between an adult-*initiated* activity and an adult-*directed* activity? Which fits the HighScope approach and which fits your approach?
   - In reviewing your last adult-initiated activity, what worked, what did not work so well and what changes might you make?

5. Transitions
   - Are there any transitions in your daily routine that you would like to review so that the day has balance, flow and momentum?
   - What successful strategies for transitions, as children move from one part of the routine to the next, can you share with others?

References

Berry, C. F., & Sylva, K. (1987) The Plan-Do-Review Cycle in HighScope: Its Effect on Children and Staff. Unpublished manuscript (available from HighScope Educational Research Foundation, Ypsilanti, MI).

Schweinhart, L. J. et al. (2005) *Life Time Effects. The HighScope Perry Preschool Study through Age 40*. Ypsilanti, MI: HighScope Press

Related reading

Boisvert, C., & Gainsley, S. (2008) *50 Activities for Large Groups. Explore and Learn Quick Cards.* Ypsilanti, MI: HighScope Press

Epstein, A. S. (2010) *Story Starters for Group Times.* Ypsilanti, MI: HighScope Press

Evans, Betsy (2007) *I Know What's Next: Preschool Transitions without Tears or Turmoil.* Ypsilanti, MI: HighScope Press

Gainsley, S. (2008) *From Message to Meaning – Using a Daily Message Board in the Preschool Classroom.* Ypsilanti, MI: HighScope Press

Graves, M. (1997) *100 Small Group Experiences,* Teachers' Idea Book 3. Ypsilanti, MI: HighScope Press

Graves, M. (2007) *80 Activities for Small Groups. Explore and Learn Quick Cards.* Ypsilanti, MI: HighScope Press

HighScope Early Childhood Staff (2009) *Small Group Times to Scaffold Early Learning,* Teachers' Idea Book Series. Ypsilanti, MI: HighScope Press

Vogel, N. (2001) *Making the Most of Plan-Do-Review,* Teachers' Idea Book 5. Ypsilanti, MI: HighScope Press

6 Adult–child interaction

A supportive interpersonal climate is essential for active learning, because active learning is a social, interactive process. Thus, the essence of High-Scope is the way adults interact with children, and this chapter will take what is the least tangible aspect of the curriculum to show how High-Scope has defined concrete strategies to relate principles like 'shared control' to practice. Starting with the nature and effects of different inter-action styles, it draws out the key elements of a supportive climate, and interaction strategies that encourage active learning. It explains the ratio-nale for using encouragement rather than praise and the six steps to a problem-solving approach to resolving interpersonal conflicts. From the central principle of active learning, this chapter will go deeper into the aspects of HighScope's fifth ingredient of 'support' or 'adult scaffolding'.

Adult–child interaction – the key to quality

The way we interact has a direct impact on relationships and learning. Time and time again, research and guidance points to adult–child inter-action as the key to quality. For example, *The Study of Pedagogical Effectiveness in Early Learning* (Moyles, Adams & Musgrove, 2002) states:

> All previous research and evaluation projects conducted in the UK and inter-nationally point conclusively to the quality of the interaction between practitioners and children in the 3–5 years age range as critical to effective curriculum imple-mentation and the long term successful outcomes of children's early learning. For example, there is increasing interest in the components of effectiveness in early

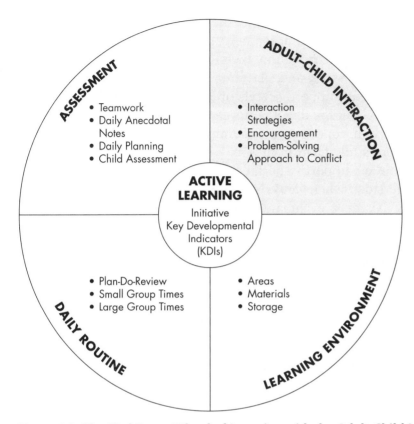

Figure 6.1 The HighScope Wheel of Learning with the Adult–Child Interaction section highlighted

Source: Hohmann, Weikart and Epstein (2008, p. 6)

years practices from such examples as the Te Whariki (New Zealand), High-Scope (USA) and Reggio Emilia approaches (Northern Italy).

The Early Years Foundation Stage (2007) *Positive Relationships 2.3 Supporting Learning* states:

Warm, trusting relationships with knowledgeable adults support children's learning more effectively than any amount of resources.

Styles of interaction

The HighScope curriculum is organised to provide a supportive and democratic climate where adults and children share control of the

learning process. Practitioners balance the freedom children need in order
to explore with the limits children need in order to feel secure. A major
goal of the HighScope curriculum, therefore, is to create an environment
where children can work and play free of fear, anxiety and boredom.
Having a consistent, supportive style of interaction, both across the staff
team and throughout the day in adult- and child-initiated activities, is a
hallmark of a HighScope setting. Relationships are warm and responsive
and, as partners, adults share in children's interests, delights and creativity.

The qualities of supportive social climates in early childhood settings
are best understood when viewed in contrast to the qualities of two other
climates: the 'laissez-faire climate' and the 'directive climate'. In a laissez-
faire climate, children are in control. There is little structure to the classroom or daily routine. Practitioners make sure children are safe and take
care of children's basic needs, but otherwise they leave children free to
play as they wish. At the other end of this continuum, in a directive climate it is the adults who are in control. They tell the children what to do
and when to do it, often using scripted lessons to teach specific academic

Table 6.1 Contrasting climates for children

Laissez-faire	Supportive	Directive
Children are in control most of the time, with adults as bystanders who provide supervision.	Children and adults have control.	Adults are in control.
Adults intervene to respond to requests, offer information, restore order.	Adults observe children's strengths, form authentic partnerships with children, support children's intentional play.	Adults give directions and information.
Curriculum content comes from children's play.	Curriculum content comes from children's initiatives and is designed with the KDIs in mind.	Curriculum content comes from learning objectives set by adults.
Adults highly value children's play.	Adults highly value children's active learning.	Adults highly value drill and practice for children.
Adults use various approaches to child management.	Adults take a problem-solving approach to social conflict.	Adults use correction and separation as predominant child management strategies.

Source: Hohmann, Weikart and Epstein, 2008, p. 49

skills and concepts. In an early years setting, often child-initiated periods of the day lean towards a laissez-faire climate and adult-initiated or directed towards a directive climate.

The key elements of support

HighScope has developed six key elements of support as guidelines for working with children. These key elements of support describe characteristics children will remember their practitioners by, adults whose company they liked being in and whom they found emotionally nourishing.

Adults create supportive climates that encourage the development of young children's capacities for trust, autonomy, initiative, empathy and self-confidence, which are identified in child development literature as building blocks of children's social and emotional health (Erikson, 1950).

These six elements are:

- sharing control between both adults and children
- focusing on children's strengths
- forming authentic relationships with children
- making a commitment to supporting children's play
- using encouragement instead of praise
- adopting a problem-solving approach to social conflict.

Together with the ingredients of active learning, the elements of support provide a guiding framework for the HighScope curriculum which influences every other aspect of the approach.

These key elements of support will be present as characteristics in any positive situation. In the HighScope curriculum they come into play throughout the day whenever adults and children are interacting.

Sharing control between both adults and children

Shared control is central to how adults and children interact in the High-Scope approach. Practitioners are learning about children's individual interests, strengths and abilities and children are learning from working in an environment that adults have planned and arranged for their learning. There is an atmosphere of mutual respect. Again, shared control is an abstract concept, and to link principles to practice HighScope has many general and specific strategies for accomplishing this goal, so that the fear of losing control is eliminated.

This means that in a HighScope setting materials are accessible to children and there is a balance between child- and adult-initiated activities in the daily routine. Each room has a daily routine chart (see Chapter 5, pages 98–100) so children can see what comes next, and use of the message board after greeting time (see Chapter 5, pages 89–91) shares information about the day ahead. Practitioners follow children's lead in play and conversation and notice children's work by making descriptive comments. They ask children for solutions in both physical and social problem-solving situations and share their observations with parents.

Focusing on children's strengths

HighScope recognises the uniqueness of each child and develops every individual's self-confidence by the starting-point for learning being what the child *can* do. By beginning with what children can do and what they are interested in, the motivation to learn is built in. Focusing on children's strengths is key to individualised learning, and practitioners are consciously thinking about how to support the learning of each child.

This means that in a HighScope setting one sees observations which focus on what children can do. Daily planning for small group time and large group time and strategies for planning time, recall time and tidy-up time regularly follow children's interests. Practitioners pay close attention to children's interests, realising that they may not be the repetitive play they at first thought.

Forming authentic relationships with children

Children are very adept at picking up adult nuances and seem to instinctively sense genuine attention. This occurs naturally where practitioners enjoy their work, are excited by following children's interests and note their emerging abilities.

This means that in a HighScope setting practitioners share their interests with children. The practitioners speak in their natural voice and are themselves. There will be smiles, hugs, eye contact and getting down to children's level. In conversations, practitioners listen attentively, ask honest questions, answer questions honestly and give specific feedback instead of 'empty' praise. They show enthusiasm.

Supporting children's play

'Playing with princesses and playdough as partners with children' is a key part of the practitioner's role during work time; it is not only valid but essential. HighScope agrees with the idea that play is a child's work, hence the terminology 'work time' for child-initiated play. Whatever form play takes – noisy or quiet, messy or orderly, silly or serious, and effortful or easy – play is a time when a great deal of learning takes place.

This means that in a HighScope setting there are practitioners who are available to play and converse with children. They play as partners with children, joining in without taking over, offering suggestions within the play theme and respecting the child's reaction to their ideas. HighScope practitioners are playful with children.

Using encouragement instead of praise

Many adults use praise because they think it helps children to feel good about themselves and their work. They may also use praise as a behaviour-management tool to help children settle down and be 'well behaved'. However, praise can actually be damaging because children learn to depend on adults to figure out what is right or wrong, instead of developing this ability themselves. Use of praise also invites children to perform for external rewards rather than to embrace learning for its own sake. For these reasons, HighScope practitioners use encouragement rather than praise to recognise children's accomplishments and support their inherent interest in learning. For more on encouragement instead of praise, see pages 119–22 later in this chapter.

Adopting a problem-solving approach

The problem-solving approach to conflict is a long-term strategy that supportive adults can use with children of any age. The children work through the steps described later in this chapter with the support of an adult in order to resolve conflicts that arise during the daily routine. When children practise resolving social conflicts from an early age, by the time they reach adulthood they have many of the social skills they need, the habit of using them and the confidence gained from years of experience and support.

The practical strategies of a problem-solving approach to conflict are described in this chapter on pages 123–4.

A supportive climate for family involvement

HighScope practitioners use the key elements of support to guide their interactions with children's families and address issues and problems that arise. A supportive climate for family involvement is characterised by shared control between children and adults and a partnership between parents and practitioners, a focus on children's and families' strengths, authenticity on the part of adults, a commitment to family-inspired play and a problem-solving approach to conflict resolution. With the partnership relationship as the primary focus, practitioners' understanding of children and their families enriches the sense of belonging and well-being for everyone.

Effective communication

Motivational theorists suggest that children (in fact all learners) are most likely to become involved or motivated in activities and interactions that are enjoyable, that are related to their current needs and interests, and that allow them to experience feelings of control and success.

(Powell, 1991 p. 29).

HighScope practitioners think consciously about interaction strategies that are congruent with a democratic interaction style. These have been defined by analysing the way practitioners who just naturally engage with children communicate, and are then practised by all practitioners. Using the principle of intrinsic motivation or the question, 'What makes a learner?' guides HighScope practitioners in using the following strategies:

- looking for children in need of comfort and contact
- participating in children's play
- conversing with children
- encouraging children's problem solving.

Looking for children in need of comfort and contact
Practitioners look out for children who are expressing anxiety or discomfort, watching others play, moving quickly from one thing to another, or frequently asking for an adult. They will support these children by offering a hand to hold, a lap to curl up in, reassuring arms around them or just an adult's calm presence near by. Occasionally all that is needed is

acknowledgement of children's efforts, which can be a simple nod, a smile or a comment.

Participating in children's play

Practitioners look for natural play openings. It is easier and less disruptive to join children's exploratory play (for example, squeezing dough, pouring water, finger painting), pretend play (for example, being a party guest, putting the baby figure to bed in the dolls' house, pretending to drive cars down a block road) or games (for example, simple card games children make up), rather than their constructive play (for example, building a block road, painting a picture, making a Duplo tower). Practitioners kneel, sit and lie on the floor so that they are on the same physical level as the children. Sometimes practitioners play in parallel with children by simply playing near them using the same materials in the same way. Sometimes they play as a partner with children, which works well in pretend play or games. Practitioners look for opportunities to refer one child to another, enabling children to use their own abilities for the benefit of others, recognise one another's strengths, regard one another as a valuable resource and play co-operatively. Practitioners may also challenge young children's thinking to expand their play and understanding by offering suggestions within the children's play themes, addressing the roles rather than the children themselves. For example, addressing the mummy or the puppy dog that a child is pretending to be, yet all the time respecting the child's reactions to their ideas.

Conversing with children

Practitioners are available for conversations throughout the day, encouraging children to talk because they feel that adults enjoy these conversations. They will be prepared for any subject – the past, things from the classroom, things that happen at home, speculations about the future or imaginings, and will respond to children's chosen topics with interested comments and honest questions. They sit, kneel, or crouch down so that they are at the same level as the children, who then know they have the practitioner's full attention. By being silent yet attentive and listening patiently and with interest they can respond to children's conversational leads.

In conversing as a partner with children, practitioners will pass control of the conversation back to children at every opportunity. This means sticking to the topics children raise, making comments that allow the conversation to continue without pressuring children for a response, waiting for children to respond before taking another turn and keeping comments fairly brief. HighScope practitioners are trained to ask questions responsively and sparingly so that children retain control of the conversation. This means that they relate questions directly to what children are doing instead of asking questions about facts the practitioner already knows, like "What colour is that?" "How many do you have?" They ask questions about children's thought processes, which encourages children to talk about what they are thinking. For example, "How can you tell?" "What do you think made that happen?" "How did you get the ball to. . .?" "What do you think would happen if. . .?" "What will you try next?"

Encouraging children's problem solving
Practitioners look for children involved in problem-solving situations and allow children to deal with problems and conflicting viewpoints if they can. They will interact with, rather than manage, children and assist matter-of-factly with unresolved conflict. They will show patience and respect, and be non-judgemental and support the children in engaging in the problem-solving approach so that they can learn the skills necessary to be problem solvers themselves. HighScope has defined the six steps to conflict resolution that are described in this chapter on pages 123–4.

Scaffolding children's learning

'Adult scaffolding' is the fifth practical ingredient of active learning and therefore central to the HighScope approach. The detail of how to apply this to practice encompasses the styles and strategies described throughout this chapter and highlighted as key principles in the adult–child interaction section of the Wheel of Learning on page 111. It is by using these interaction strategies throughout all parts of the daily routine that HighScope practitioners scaffold each child's learning to match his or her stage of development. Successful scaffolding takes play from being reactive and random, to intentional, purposeful and mature. This adds to children's innate imagination, invention and rich vocabulary in a meaningful context.

Scaffolding has been derived from the work of the Russian theorist Lev Vygotsky and his work on the Zone of Proximal Development, which he defined as 'the gap between what a child can do independently and what he can do with support from an adult or more capable peers' (Mooney, 2000 p. 83).

HighScope's definition of scaffolding means to:

- support children's current levels of development and
- provide gentle extensions as they move to the next developmental stage.

In this way, practitioners work with children to help them gain knowledge, develop creative problem-solving skills and reflect on what they are learning. For example, they observe and imitate children's actions, repeat the words they use and extend their vocabularies, and pose open-ended questions that encourage children to try new things and consider the 'what, how and why' of their experiences. Practitioners also refer children to one another to share ideas and solve problems collaboratively. Their availability to scaffold children's learning throughout adult- and child-initiated parts of the daily routine is essential.

Praise versus encouragement

In a HighScope setting you will not see any reward stickers or charts or hear praise statements like "excellent", "well done", "I am very pleased with you", and the children do not need these external motivators in order to behave or have high levels of involvement in their work.

Praise and extrinsic rewards conflict with HighScope principles of shared control and intrinsic motivation, which value children engaging in learning because they want to and not to please someone else, usually an authority figure.

HighScope has identified the following negative implications of praise and believes that it:

- makes children dependent on adults
- takes away children's power to evaluate their own work
- has a negative effect on self-esteem
- can produce a classroom of 'praise junkies'
- causes anger and resentment when used to manage or manipulate
- discourages risk taking
- lessens self-motivation, discourages problem solving.

HighScope Educational Consultant Mark Thompkins (1991) notes that:

> Praise, well intentioned as it might be, has been shown through research and practice to invite comparison and competition and to increase the child's dependence on adults. Too much praise can make children anxious about their abilities, reluctant to take risks and try new things and unsure of how to evaluate their own efforts.

Encouragement is used as the alternative to praise in HighScope settings. It shows children that practitioners notice their accomplishments and respect their efforts. It allows children to feel they can make mistakes and learn from them without being judged. HighScope practitioners accomplish this by using three basic strategies:

- *They participate in children's play*
  Practitioners get involved in children's play, observe what they are doing and saying and are responsive to children's actions and interests.

- *They encourage children to describe their efforts and products*
  Practitioners encourage reflective thinking by asking open-ended questions, repeating what children say and listening carefully.

- *They acknowledge children's work or ideas by making specific comments*
  Practitioners notice the details in the work, and comment on them without making a judgement.

In short, HighScope practitioners take off their 'judge's hat' and stay with what they see and label and describe. They notice and give attention to children's work and achievements. One hears comments like these: "You spent a long time on that picture", "You've used red, blue and green paint", "Thank you for cleaning the table", "How did you build your animal hospital, Ellie?" "You put your shoes on by yourself".

Their actions can be encouraging too; a nod or a smile sends a message of encouragement, as does listening without interrupting.

The belief that encouragement is more effective than praise stems from two different educational theories: behaviourist and constructivist. Behaviourism is a theory of how children and adults learn that was devised by John B. Watson at the turn of the century and popularised by B. F. Skinner. The belief is that behaviour is shaped by reinforcement, in other words, when a behaviour is rewarded it is likely to be repeated. This basic strategy can be summed up in six words: 'Do *this* and you'll get *that*'. *This* relates to an action, task or work and *that* relates to a reward. It relies on extrinsic motivation, an inducement outside of the task itself, and is controlled by an authority figure. 'Behaviourism' has been widely taught as a model of behaviour management and is embedded in societies around the world in nurseries, schools, homes and the workplace. In the early years this appears as golden rules, celebration assemblies, merit awards, stickers, reward charts and refrains of 'good sitting', 'good listening'.

Constructivism is the theory of learning derived largely from the work of Piaget and Dewey. It encompasses all the ingredients of active learning and its natural outcomes of intrinsic motivation and curriculum content (KDIs).

Constructivism believes that children learn actively by doing things for themselves. They construct new knowledge by thinking about what they already know and working through problems, on their own and with others, and thereby coming to understanding. In a setting that holds true to constructivism, there are lots of opportunities for children to explore, discover, think and be creative without a fear of making mistakes or being judged. They will talk about their experiences with attentive adults and peers, and problem solving, decision making, initiative and independence are highly valued.

HighScope's belief in the constructivist theory of education is clearly seen in its definition of active participatory learning (see Chapter 3, page 33):

> Active participatory learning is defined as learning in which the child, by acting on objects and interacting with people, ideas and events, constructs new understanding. No one else can have experiences for the child or construct knowledge for the child. Children must do this for themselves.
>
> Hohmann, Weikart and Epstein (2008 p. 17)

HighScope's practical ingredients of active participatory learning (see Chapter 3, pages 37–8) set the conditions that lead to children's intrinsic motivation or personal initiative.

Changing from using praise to encouragement can be difficult when praise is such an automatic response and there is sometimes a fine line between the two. Alfie Kohn (1999) describes two criteria that are helpful in distinguishing between the two:

■ *Self-determination*
Are we helping the child feel a sense of control over his or her life, make his or her own judgements and choose what kind of person to be? Or are we attempting to manipulate or control behaviour by getting the child to think about whether he or she has met our criteria?

■ *Intrinsic motivation*
Are we creating conditions for the child to become more deeply involved in what he or she is doing – or turning the task into something the child does to win our approval?

A problem-solving approach to conflict

Taken together, encouragement and a problem-solving approach to conflict provide an alternative in HighScope settings to 'behaviour management'. The emphasis is on *interaction* rather than *management*.

In HighScope settings, practitioners view social conflict as an opportunity to teach social and emotional life skills, and they accept conflict as a healthy, normal part of learning and human development. They see supporting conflict resolution as an everyday part of their adult role and a valuable learning opportunity; this attitude changes the negative feelings associated with conflict to more positive feelings associated with problem solving.

Preventing classroom conflicts

Many problems are prevented or at least reduced by using the HighScope guidelines regarding active learning, the physical environment, the daily routine, adult–child interaction, observation and daily planning, and are summarised in Box 6.1

Box 6.1 Preventing classroom conflicts

The following characteristics of the HighScope curriculum help to prevent problems and conflicts from happening in the classroom:

- spacious work areas with enough materials for all children
- predictable daily routine
- children carrying out their own plans during work time
- children having choices during group times and transitions
- group activities planned around children's interests
- little or no waiting before getting started on activities
- adults helping children to identify and express their feelings
- adults making daily observations and anecdotal notes about children.

Taken from *Essentials of Active Learning in Preschool: Getting to Know the HighScope Curriculum* by Ann S. Epstein

The six steps to conflict resolution

When conflicts arise, HighScope practitioners use the six steps to conflict resolution described in detail in Evans (2002). They do not always go in this order and some steps may need to be repeated. There will often be an emphasis on Step 2 of the process, 'Acknowledging feelings' and on Step 5, 'Asking children for solutions to the problem'.

To resolve conflict practitioners will:

1. Approach calmly, stopping any hurtful actions
   Place themselves between children, on their level
   - Watch their tone of voice
   - Quickly and gently stop any hurting

2. Acknowledge children's feelings
   For example, they might say "You look really upset"
   - Place their hands on the disputed object and say "I'm going to hold this until we figure out the problem". They will keep the object in view
   - Look at each child and use the children's names
   - Name feelings repeatedly until children are calmer

3. Gather information
   For example, they might ask, "What's the problem?"
   - Ask "what", not "why"
   - Listen for the details of the problem

4. Restate the problem

For example, they might say "So the problem is. . ."

- Restate the details that they hear in the children's words
- Reframe any hurtful comments, set limits on hurtful actions if necessary, naming the feelings message ("Name calling needs to stop. You are feeling very angry.")

5. Ask for ideas for solutions and choose one together

For example, they might say "What can we do to solve this problem?"

- Encourage *children's* ideas for solutions
- Ask other children for ideas, if necessary
- When ideas are vague, ask "What will that look like?" or "What will you do?"

6. Be prepared to give follow-up support

For example they might say "You solved the problem!"

- Describe what the child did that worked, with details
- Check back to make sure the solution is still working

Children will be heard using the language of problem solving, like "problem" and "solution", that is modelled to them on a daily basis, and will need less adult intervention, or none at all. With younger children, less verbally able children or children with English as an additional language, the adults will describe what they see and observe, offer ideas for solutions or ask older children near by for their ideas. Otherwise, the six steps to conflict resolution apply to all age groups, from babies through to senior citizens.

Key points

1. In the HighScope curriculum shared control is central to how adults and children interact.
2. HighScope recognises the uniqueness of each child and develops his self-confidence by the starting-point for learning being what he *can* do.
3. Practitioners play as partners with children, joining children at their level, following their leads and taking turns in play and conversation.
4. Children are most likely to become involved or motivated in activities and interactions that are enjoyable, that are related to their

current needs and interests and that allow them to experience feelings of control and success.

5. Ask questions responsively and sparingly, avoiding 'test type' questions like "What colour is it?"
6. Effective styles and strategies of interaction 'scaffold' children's learning and development, giving an underlying sense of self-esteem, well-being and opportunities for more complex play.
7. Research shows that there are many drawbacks to using praise and rewards as ways to motivate young children.
8. Encouragement fosters intrinsic motivation to learn and is descriptive rather than evaluative.
9. Supporting children's problem solving is a key adult role which teaches important social and emotional life skills.
10. In a problem-solving approach adults interact with rather than manage children.

Reflections on the HighScope approach

1. Contrasting climates for children
   - Who is in control in your classroom?
   - Does this shift from one part of the day to another?
   - In what ways can you share control with children?
2. Supporting children's learning
   - How would you like children you work with now to remember you in 25 years' time?
   - What characteristics or traits do people you have found supportive have?
3. Partners in play
   - How did you like to play when you were a child?
   - If the 'ideal' adult had joined you in play, what would you have wanted them to do?
4. Motivation to learn
   - What external motivators do you use?
   - What internal motivators do you use?
   - What is the impact on children?
5. Conflict resolution
   - What methods do you use to resolve conflicts?
   - What does this teach the children?
   - How were conflicts resolved when you were a child?

References

Erikson, E. (1950) *Childhood and Society*. New York: Norton

Evans, B. (2002) *You Can't Come to My Birthday Party. Conflict Resolution with Young Children*. Ipsilanti MI: HighScope Press

Hohmann, M., Weikart, D. P., & Epstein, A. (2008) *Educating Young Children. The Complete Guide to the HighScope Preschool Curriculum* (3rd edn). Ypsilanti, MI: HighScope Press

Mooney, C. (2000) *Theories of Childhood. An Introduction to Dewey, Montessori, Erikson, Piaget and Vygotsky*. Minnesota: Redleaf Press

Moyles, J., Adams, S., & Musgrove, A. (2002) *SPEEL Study of Pedagogical Effectiveness in Early Learning*. School of Education Research and Development, Anglia Polytechnic University

Powell, A. (1991) Be responsive! In N. A. Brickman & L. S. Taylor (eds) *Supporting Young Learners: Ideas for Preschool and Day Care Providers* (pp. 26–34). Ypsilanti, MI: HighScope Press

Thompkins, M. (1996) In Praise of Praising Less. In N. A. Brickman & L. S. Taylor (eds) *Supporting Young Learners* (pp. 5–22). Ypsilanti, MI: HighScope Press

The Early Years Foundation Stage (2007) *Principles into Practice Cards Positive Relationships 2.2 Supporting Learning*. Nottingham: Department for Education and Skills

Related reading

Biddulph, S. (1988) *The Secret of Happy Children*. Sydney and London: Bay Books

Biddulph, S. (1998) *More Secrets of Happy Children*. Sydney: Harper Collins

Evans, B. (2009) *You're not My Friend Anymore!* Ypsilanti, MI: HighScope Press

Faber, A., & Mazlish, E. (1982) *How to Teach so Kids will Listen and Listen so Kids will Talk*. New York: Avon Books

Faber, A., & Mazlish, E. (1996) *How to Talk so Kids Can Learn at Home and in School*. New York: Fireside

Faber, A., & Mazlish, E. (1998) *Siblings without Rivalry*. New York: Avon Books

Jensen, E. (1998) *Teaching with the Brain in Mind*. Alexandria, VA: Association for Supervision and Curriculum Development

Kohn, A. (1999) *Punished by Rewards. The Trouble with Gold Stars, Incentive Plans, A's, Praise and Other Bribes*. Boston and New York: Houghton Mifflin Company

Kohn, A. (2005) *Unconditional Parenting: Moving from Rewards and Punishment to Love and Reason*. New York: Atria Books

Skinner, B. F. (1974) *About Behaviourism*. New York: Knopf

Sokolov, I. & Hutton, D. (1988) *The Parent's Book: Getting on Well with Our Children*. Wellingborough: Thorsons

Tobin, L (1991) *What Do You Do with a Child Like This? Inside the Lives of Troubled Children.* Duluth, Minnesota: Whole Person Associates

Watson, J. B. (1928) *Psychological Care of Infant and Child.* New York: Norton

Watson, J. B. (1930) *Behaviourism* (rev. edn). Chicago: University of Chicago Press

7 Assessment and teamwork

Assessment in HighScope is twofold and includes both formative and summative child assessment and an assessment of curriculum practices. This chapter begins by describing how HighScope practitioners work in teams so that they can work together most effectively. It then looks at how the team assesses its work by taking anecdotal observations as the starting-point for the daily planning process and child assessment. Finally, it describes how teams maintain and develop curriculum practices using HighScope's curriculum assessment tools, the Programme Implementation Profile and Observation/Feedback.

Teamwork

In HighScope, teamwork is seen as integral to assessment because assessment includes an evaluation of everything the team does. There is a whole-team responsibility involved in the assessment cycle of observing-recording-sharing-planning children's developmental progression and evaluating curriculum practices, as these are key functions carried out by the team. The HighScope principles and processes of working with children apply equally to working with adults. The ingredients of active learning, plan-do-review, the key elements of support and a problem-solving approach to conflict are all used to generate ideas and resolve differences amongst adults in the classroom, at team meetings and during in-service training. At its best, teamwork is a process of active participatory learning that calls for a supportive climate and mutual respect.

Teams in the early years are complex social systems and consist of a variety of people in a variety of roles. Primarily, a HighScope team

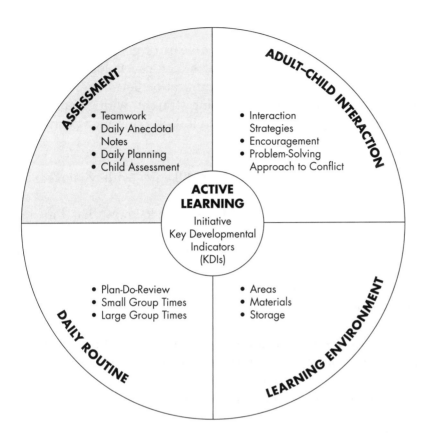

Figure 7.1 The HighScope Wheel of Learning with the Assessment section highlighted

Source: Hohmann, Weikart and Epstein (2008, p. 6)

consists of practitioners who are responsible for taking care of children and communicating with their families every day. Other team members who may also have regular contact with children or families include managers and head teachers, administrators, parent volunteers, bus drivers, cooks, cleaners and those who support the direct services, such as curriculum specialists, trainers and advisers. HighScope teams draw on the following characteristics of effective teams in order to serve children and families well.

The result of HighScope's teamwork model is seeing staff members whose enthusiasm grows from their strong belief in active participatory learning practices, and a management system where there is shared control and autonomy.

■ *Communicate openly*

Simple, honest communication is at the heart of good working relationships. HighScope draws on the work of psychologist Virginia Satir (1988), who calls such direct communication 'levelling'. In everyday language, this might be called 'being straight' with one another. This is in contrast to unhelpful communication patterns, which Satir describes as:

Placating: "No matter what I think or feel, I'll agree with whatever she wants."

Blaming: "I'll find fault with her idea so she'll know that I'm not someone she can push around."

Computing: "I'll use a lot of jargon so she'll be impressed by how much I know."

Distracting: "I'll change the subject so we don't have to deal with this uncomfortable issue."

For example, if a classroom team were discussing a problem situation during the transition of 3-year-olds from the classroom to the cloakroom to get ready for outside time, these are five different ways practitioners would communicate their concerns:

Placating: "I'll go with whatever you decide is best."

Blaming: "These children are wild."

Computing: "These children are expressing their kinaesthetic intelligence by using locomotor movements on the settee."

Distracting: "I'm going to have puzzles at my small group time this afternoon."

Levelling: "I'm worried that the children are not safe during the transition from the classroom to the cloakroom. How can we meet our need for safety and the children's need for action during transitions?"

In the HighScope approach the first four examples are seen as barriers to effective communication and only the fifth example, levelling, is helpful.

■ *Respect individual differences*

In the HighScope model of teamwork, differences in ideas, preferences and personalities are seen as a source of creativity and variation. HighScope has drawn on Likert and Lippitt's management studies, which show, for example, that a major human asset in productive teams is the 'capacity to use differences for purposes of innovation and improvement, rather than allowing differences to develop into bitter, irreconcilable, interpersonal conflict' (Likert, 1967 p. 135). Similarly, human resource developer Gordon Lippitt (1980 p. 14) points out that 'in an effective group, persons are willing to express their differences openly. Such expressions create authentic communication and more alternatives for a quality decision.'

In a HighScope setting practitioners view one another as valuable resources for gaining a broader perspective on educating young children and working with others.

■ *Have patience with the team work process*
Early childhood teams are dynamic, with changing members, changing children and families to work with. HighScope believes that the teamwork process will go back and forth with these changes, through various stages of development, to become a performing and productive team, and that this takes time and patience. HighScope aims to have all members of the team working together in a unified way and understanding the rationale for its principles and beliefs.

Box 7.1 Characteristics of an effective team

1. Climate: There is a positive climate of mutual sharing and trust. Staff and administrators know what is expected of them.
2. Goal setting: Staff work together to set goals. The goals then drive the team.
3. Expectations: Expectations are clear and are based on a shared philosophy and set of goals.
4. Decision making: Whenever possible, staff make decisions by consensus. They discuss many alternatives. Once a decision is made, everyone commits to carrying it out.
5. Handling conflict: Problems are viewed as a normal part of working together. Staff use conflict-resolution strategies to solve problems effectively.
6. Regular evaluation of teamwork: All members work together to achieve team goals. Programme evaluation is based on whether the team as a whole has achieved the group's goals.

Taken from *Essentials of Active Learning in Preschool: Getting to Know the HighScope Curriculum* by Ann S. Epstein

Daily anecdotal observations

A unifying task supporting HighScope teamwork is taking daily anecdotal observations of children. As the word 'anecdotal' suggests, these
are brief descriptions of something a child has done or said that is significant to his development. Throughout the day HighScope practitioners
will look out for these memorable occurrences and record them so they
are not forgotten. They are mindful of what John Dewey (1933 p. 193)
said, that 'observation is exploration, inquiry for the sake of discovering
something previously hidden and unknown'. Practitioners observe and
interact to get to know children.

Uses of daily anecdotal observations

Anecdotal observations are the starting-point for team planning and the
assessment process and are the main way HighScope practitioners make
decisions for children to ensure that plans match their interests, relate to
the KDIs and are developmentally appropriate. They are used to monitor
children's individual progress and the breadth and balance of children's
learning, to inform the next day's planning and to share children's progress with parents. It is these observations that demonstrate what is
happening in the setting and, thereby, evidence that practitioners are
meeting the aims of the curriculum.

Objective anecdotes

In order to gather accurate information about children and ensure
consistency, HighScope practitioners are taught to write anecdotes that
are as objective as possible. For example, they will focus on what the
child did and said (this focuses on what he can do, not what he can't do):
'Held pencil using a whole-hand grasp', vs 'Didn't hold pencil correctly'.
Observations will be factual (not subjective or evaluative): 'Smiled and
took Amy's hand', vs 'Was happy to see her friends'. They will be specific
(not general): 'Climbed up and jumped off the climber 8 times', vs 'Was
active on playground', and will be brief but with enough information to
paint a picture for someone else to understand in six months' time.

There is a consistent format for anecdotes in order to guide practitioners in this process. Each anecdote will be dated; will have a beginning identifying the context, where and when it took place; will have a

middle, describing what the child did and said; and an ending which, when applicable, states the outcome. These characteristics are shown in the following example:

23.11.10

At tidy-up time (TUT) in the art area (AA) Mia wiped painting table cloth, then table, then got sponge from shelf and gave to John to help her.

Recording observations

All practitioners record observations on any of the children and pass these to the child's key person, who has the responsibility to record the information formally on that child's observation record sheet. The observation record sheet is divided into the KDI headings and each observation is recorded under the most relevant one. In some cases an anecdote may be cross-referenced to cover two areas. Practitioners use abbreviations and capture the information on post-it notes, on clip boards, in notebooks, with cameras or tape recorders. Whatever method is chosen, there will be the means to note the anecdote as soon as possible. Practitioners set a realistic goal for the number of anecdotes to record, which will generally be four or five a day.

In addition to written observation records, it is usual for HighScope practitioners to collect samples of work and photographs and to store these in individual portfolios to which children have access. These records will be passed through the setting and given to the child when they leave, to share with their school.

Daily team planning

HighScope planning is characterised by its simplicity. The emphasis is on planning daily, so that the team can turn the successes and problems of one day's work into the plans and strategies for the next day, with the team meaning both practitioners and assistants, illustrating the principle of shared control.

Observation record sheet

Child __Lily__   Date of Birth __4.8.06__
Observer __Elsa__

Remember to date all entries

Approaches to Learning	Social and Emotional Development	Physical Development and Health	Language, Literacy and Communication
19/7/10 LGT said "I have an idea, we could all be hippos rolling in the mud"	13/6/10 ST said "Greg only likes bananas, please save one for him"	22/7/10 SGT used scissors to cut a 'fringe' along the side of paper	26/6/10 AA at WT said "go flo blow, they all sound the same"
8/8/10 WT AA spent all of WT making a castle using paper, tape and markers	12/7/10 GT runs up to Noah, gives him a hug and says "Noah, I've missed you the whole day"	29/7/10 OT for the first time managed to use her legs to make the swing go	29/6/10 BA at WT was sitting looking at a story book and telling a story from the pictures
7/9/10 PT said "First I am going to the art area to use the new envelopes, then I want to play in the sand and then I want to read the Dora book"	8/8/10 Holds Elliot's hand throughout the photography session after noticing that he is uncomfortable with the situation	30/7/10 WT was walking around the nursery on all fours swaying from side to side being an elephant	12/9/10 WT went over to the cubbies and wrote down each child's name on her piece of paper. Then said "I can check off who goes home today"

Figure 7.2 Observation record sheet

Source: Pro forma supplied by HighScope Educational Research Foundation.

Observation record sheet

Child __Lily__   Date of Birth __4.8.06__
Observer __Elsa__

Remember to date all entries

Mathematics	Creative Arts	Science and Technology	Social Studies
18/7/10 ST held up a triangle shaped piece of pineapple and said "like a triangle"	18/7/10 HA at WT pretended to give the teddies their medicine, change their nappies and put them to bed	20/7/10 SGT playing with the plastic animals and making the appropriate sounds for horse, cow and pig	18/7/10 PT said "If you want to find me later, I'll be in the book area"
4/8/10 SGT cut the dough into 4 pieces and said "I've made 4 cakes"	14/8/10 LGT Chose a tambourine and played it in a steady beat to the music	14/8/10 AA at WT comparing paint brushes said "Mine's larger and fatter than yours"	3/8/10 LGT said "I know, lets sing Auntie Monica"
6/8/10 WT in the BA counted 7 penguins accurately on a friend's jumper		10/9/10 RT said "see my picture, I mixed red and white and got pink"	16/8/10 WT drew a map of treasure island and marked the road with a black line and the treasure in a yellow circle

Figure 7.2 Continued

Planning around the daily routine

With the literal definition of 'planning' as 'thought before action', ideally planning will take place every day. HighScope uses a simple planning form based on the daily routine that is focused and should not take more than half an hour to complete. This ensures that all team members know what the others are doing, materials for small group time, large group time, planning time and recall time are gathered in advance and it is easy for relief or agency staff to fit in with a clear sense of purpose. Additionally, possible content areas are noted to ensure a broad and balanced curriculum. The team begins by discussing anecdotes taken that day and using these to provide for everyone, but individualises learning for some children based on their interests and developmental abilities. The child observation record sheet, with anecdotes recorded under the KDI headings, will clearly reveal gaps in the curriculum that can then be planned for to provide broad coverage of the curriculum content.

Other sources for planning include the curriculum content in the KDIs, new materials to introduce to the children, the need to teach a skill or a decision to reintroduce less-used materials, for example, if the painting area hasn't been used recently.

Practitioners will turn to a Child Observation Record (COR) Assessment tool reading and related 'What's Next' ideas or any of the Teacher Idea Books and other curriculum materials that contain ideas for what to do next (see related reading at the end of this chapter). As shown in Figure 7.3, plans for transitions and tidy-up time are noted and at small group time practitioners consider what children at different developmental levels may do, and thereby anticipate ways to scaffold and individualise learning within the activity. Additionally, team members will confirm allocated responsibilities and address any issues to problem-solve.

Each team member brings unique interests and talents to the planning meeting. The same interaction principles that practitioners use with children apply between adults. HighScope recognises that it is important to let team members know their contributions are valued by using encouragement rather than praise with one another.

HighScope Demonstration Preschool Daily Plan

Date: 12.12.10

Adults: Martina and Elsa

Greeting Time:
Door: Martina
Books: Elsa
Transition: by colour of clothes

Child Messages: (1) Noah and Elliot not here today
(2) 2 no school days
(3) shells in the sand

Planning Time
Peer planning, tell a friend what you plan to do at work time

Planning Time
Tell Tom (class doll) your plan

Work Time
Support art area and painting, encourage restaurant play

Tidy-up 5 minute warning, tidy up time tickets (interest areas). Pick a ticket and tidy that area.

Recall Time
Tap a wand on something you used and show where you worked

Recall Time
Write a group recall story (dictation) of what happened at worktime in our class today

Snack: milk, pears, grapes

Large-Group Time: Easy To Join: Everybody do this
Songbook: Pamela
'Simon says' dance movements to Mama Mia CD
Content: Physical Development and Health

Transition Spaceship to small-group time

Small-Group Time
Materials: newspaper advertisements containing large numerals, scissors, markers, envelopes for collections
Content: Mathematics

Earlier	Middle	Later
explore newspaper, tear, cut, use markers, mix letters and numerals	identify numerals with some errors, cut out numerals, sort and collect in envelope	cut out numerals, line up in order, identify missing numeral, make collections

Small-Group Time
Materials: small blocks, play people, animals
Content: Language, Literary and Communication

Earlier	Middle	Later
building with blocks, moving animals and people	pretending with materials, telling story by self	telling story with parts and detail

Outside Time
Collect snow in see through jar to take inside and observe. Sledges, bats, balls and hoops

To Remember Add suitcases and small coloured blocks to BA
Parent volunteers sign up list for winter festival

Content → Interests → Planning Ideas → Developmental Range → Support Strategies

Figure 7.3 Daily team planning

Source: Pro forma supplied by HighScope Educational Research Foundation.

Child assessment

Summative assessment

To condense the formative assessment of anecdotal observations into a summative assessment, HighScope developed the Child Observation Record (COR) for preschoolers (HighScope Educational Research Foundation, 1992; 2003a) and for under-threes (HighScope, 2002). The Preschool COR assesses children aged from 2½ to 6 years and the Infant Toddler COR assesses children from 6 weeks to 3 years. Because children develop at different rates the two measures overlap in the age range covered. The COR has been designed to be used in all developmentally appropriate early childhood settings, not just those implementing the HighScope approach. As an observation-based assessment tool, it follows on from the processes of gathering anecdotal observations and daily team planning and is completed once or twice a year for each child. It enables users to look at meaningful educational outcomes, gather information in ways that are natural and comfortable for children and adults and provide accurate data that can be used for individual child planning and policy-level decision making.

How the COR is used?

The COR is a kit containing resources for practitioners to make a summative assessment either online or manually. Practitioners observe children, record anecdotes, score the COR and use this information in daily team planning, family conferences and programme evaluation.

The COR is organised into categories of development. For the Infant Toddler COR these are:

- Sense of self
- Social relations
- Creative representation
- Movement
- Communication and language
- Exploration and early logic.

For the preschool COR the categories of development are:

- Initiative
- Social relations

- Creative representation
- Movement and music
- Language and literacy
- Mathematics and science.

Within each category is a list of observation items. These items are based on the key developmental indicators. There are six categories and 28 items on the Infant Toddler COR and six categories and 32 items on the Preschool COR. Each item is designated an alphabetical symbol from A to BB on the Infant Toddler COR and from A to FF on the Preschool COR.

For each of these items there are five developmental levels that describe behaviour ranging from simple (1) to more complex (5). (Recently a '0' level has been added to the Preschool COR to facilitate the transition from the under-threes to the preschool assessment tool and to better accommodate rating children with special needs.)

Box 7.2 Categories and items on the Child Observation Record (COR)

Preschool COR

1. Initiative
A. Making choices and plans
B. Solving problems with materials
C. Initiating play
D. Taking care of personal needs

II. Social relations
E. Relating to adults
F. Relating to other children
G. Resolving interpersonal conflict
H. Understanding and expressing feelings

III. Creative representation
I. Making and building models

Infant-Toddler COR

1. Sense of self
A. Expressing initiative
B. Distinguishing self from others
C. Solving problems
D. Developing self-help skills

II. Social relations
E. Forming an attachment to a primary caregiver
F. Relating to unfamiliar adults
G. Relating to another child
H. Expressing emotion
I. Responding to the feelings of others
J. Playing with others

III. Creative representation
K. Pretending

J. Drawing and painting pictures
K. Pretending

L. Exploring building and art materials
M. Responding to and identifying pictures and photographs

IV. Movement and music
L. Moving in various ways
M. Moving with objects
N. Feeling and expressing steady beat
O. Moving to music
P. Singing

IV. Movement
N. Moving parts of the body
O. Moving the whole body
P. Moving with objects
Q. Moving to music

V. Language and literacy

Q. Listening to and understanding speech
R. Using vocabulary
S. Using complex patterns of speech
T. Showing awareness of sounds in words
U. Demonstrating knowledge about books
V. Using letter names and sounds
W. Reading
X. Writing

V. Communication and language
R. Listening and responding
S. Communicating interest nonverbally
T. Participating in give-and-take communication
U. Speaking
V. Exploring picture books
W. Showing interest in stories, rhymes, and songs

VI. Mathematics and science

Y. Sorting objects
Z. Identifying patterns
AA. Comparing properties
BB. Counting
CC. Identifying position and direction
DD. Identifying sequence, change, and causality
EE. Identifying materials and properties
FF. Identifying natural and living things

VI. Exploration and early logic
X. Exploring objects
Y. Exploring categories
Z. Developing number understanding
AA. Exploring space
BB. Exploring time

Taken from *Essentials of Active Learning in Preschool: Getting to Know the HighScope Curriculum* by Ann S. Epstein

An example of these levels is shown in the following extract, which looks at item W on the Preschool COR: Reading

- Item W Reading
    Level 1   Child uses the same word to name more than one object
    Level 2   Child says what a picture or symbol represents
    Level 3   Child calls attention to print
    Level 4   Child recognises a written word
    Level 5   Child reads aloud a simple phrase or sentence

Each item includes a short explanation, the five scoring levels and examples of anecdotes that illustrate each level. The practitioner will then score the COR by matching their anecdote to a level.

The advantages of authentic assessment

The COR is described as an authentic assessment and includes objective observations, portfolios of children's work and teacher and parent ratings of children's behaviour. It takes place within the child's familiar environment and routine and with familiar adults. As such, it provides a more accurate picture of what children normally do and reflects their true capabilities. HighScope believes that the advantages of this approach are:

- It is based on real performance of the child, rather than an artificial testing situation.
- It can focus on a broad range of developmental areas.
- It assesses thinking and problem-solving abilities, not just factual knowledge.
- It produces a profile of change and development over time.
- It helps adults to develop objective observational skills.
- It helps adults to become more knowledgeable about child development.
- It encourages programmes to view learning from a child's perspective.
- It provides child-focused information that adults can use to plan activities.
- It makes adults pay attention to the 'invisible' child.
- If it is done as part of regular on-going activities, it does not add to programme time or cost.
- It can be done by all staff, including assistants with proper training.

- It provides feedback to programme administration and funding agencies.
- It provides valuable and meaningful information for staff and parents to share, using a parents' report drawn from COR anecdotes.

HighScope validates the assessment instruments it develops to make sure they meet the same rigorous scientific standards for reliability and validity that conventional tests do. This means that a reliable assessment produces the same results when completed by different observers or at two closely spaced points in time and a valid instrument measures what it claims, is consistent with findings from similar measures and may also predict future behaviour. When developed according to these strict requirements, authentic measures can and should be as standardised as conventional tests.

Curriculum (setting) assessment

In HighScope, curriculum assessment involves practitioners in reflecting on their practice to ensure that they are meeting their stated aims. HighScope uses two techniques: the Programme Implementation Profile (UK) and Observation/Feedback. Both are observation-based assessment tools designed for practitioners to maintain and develop practice.

The Programme Implementation Profile (PIP) (UK)

The PIP is a rating scale instrument to assess where practitioners are in their implementation of HighScope and generate ideas for areas for development. It was developed in 2000 by HighScope UK as an adaptation of the Programme Quality Assessment (PQA) (HighScope Educational Research Foundation, 2003b) developed by the HighScope Educational Research Foundation (USA).

The PIP is a comprehensive assessment that looks at all aspects of programme quality and has five sections:

- A. The learning environment
- B. The daily routine
- C. Adult–child interaction
- D. Assessment
- E. Parent involvement.

There are both Preschool and Infant Toddler versions.

Each section has several items, each with a five point-scale from a low (1) to a high (5) level of quality. Descriptors under levels 1, 3 and 5 define a continuum of quality.

Scoring the PIP

The assessor observes in the classroom for a full morning or afternoon session, gathering evidence as objective observations. Supporting evidence can be materials lists, a brief note of a situation or actual language from children and adults. All supporting evidence will be objective and focus on what is in place, be descriptive and not evaluative and offer ideas, tips and suggestions for development. The assessor will underline phrases in the descriptors that reflect what is seen and finally circle the appropriate level, though if more information is needed this may not be until the feedback meeting.

A feedback meeting, lasting about 45 minutes, between the assessor and classroom staff will be held as soon as possible after the observation visit. The assessor will share her observations and invite contributions, which are then noted on the document. The assessor will facilitate a

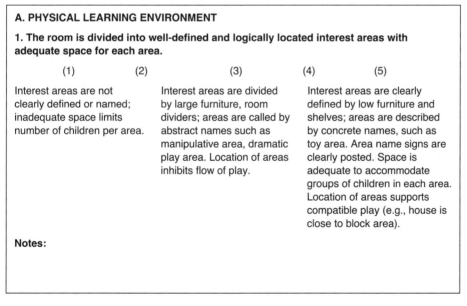

Figure 7.4 Sample item for the Programme Implementation Profile

Source: HighScope UK (2000)

reciprocal dialogue, with a sense of collaboration, on achieving what is best for children in the setting.

Uses of the PIP

The PIP will be completed by a trainer as the culmination of the High-Scope Implementation Course or at any stage of training; by a manager or curriculum specialist as staff supervision; by co-workers as peer support; or as self-assessment and monitoring on a six-monthly basis. Additionally, it can be used for research and evaluation studies and for information and dissemination of practices in high-quality programmes.

Observation/Feedback

Observation/Feedback is another curriculum assessment process used to support growth and development, used primarily by supervisors or managers but also used between peers in HighScope settings. The purpose is to provide tailor-made support by taking a small piece of the curriculum at a time and examining it together. Practitioners and managers choose the part of the curriculum that will be the focus of the observation and identify a child to observe, so that the focus is seen 'through the eyes of a child'. The focus is usually related to a recent in-service training, for example, active learning, small group time or adult support during work time. By taking small parts of the curriculum at a time, practitioners and supervisors can see how this affects the whole curriculum.

The observation lasts approximately 15–20 minutes. The observer will use a two-column narrative/notes form to record a detailed narrative of what happens and makes notes about its relevance to the curriculum focus chosen. The narrative is a factual, specific and detailed description of what happens, including the focus child's actions and language, along with other children and adults he interacts with. The notes link what the observer saw and heard to the curriculum focus and are used to stimulate dialogue with team members at the feedback meeting. They will include what struck the observer about what the focus child did or said, comments relating back to the curriculum focus and questions to clarify or extend the feedback.

The feedback meeting

The observer uses the completed narrative/notes form to discuss the observation, encouraging team members to add what they saw and heard. Using shared dialogue, the observer adds the team's contributions to her notes and makes connections to the curriculum focus. Together they interpret the observation narrative through the curriculum notes to see what makes it work. By noticing how much is in place and what they need to do, together the observer and team summarise strengths and generate and document strategies to deal with areas for development. They make follow-up plans for all team members and arrange a date for the next observation/feedback session.

HighScope believes the Observation/Feedback process is effective for several reasons:

- It is an on-going evaluation.
- It supports growth and development over time rather than enforced change.
- It is selective and deals with one area of the curriculum at a time.
- It is based on the factual, child-centred observation narrative and the curriculum-related notes.
- It approaches areas for development from strengths.
- It results in mutually generated and agreed-upon action.

Managers and practitioners work together in the classroom, looking objectively at what is working well and what is working less well in terms of outcomes for children, rather than viewing the session as a personal critique of the practitioner. Using the supporting curriculum checklist found in *Educating Young Children* (2008) keeps the process focused and objective, with a public agenda where participants can share control.

The work of the adult team follows the same principles as the work of children in the HighScope approach; in Observation/Feedback the 'review' discussion results in a 'plan' that the teachers 'do'. The focus on growth and development rather than enforced change results in intrinsic motivation rather than extrinsic motivation.

Key points

1. Teamwork, child assessment and curriculum assessment are inextricably connected.
2. The principles and processes of working with children apply equally to working with adults; this includes active learning, intrinsic motivation and the key elements of support, encouragement and a problem-solving approach to conflict.
3. The characteristics of HighScope teams are to communicate openly, respect individual differences and have patience with the teamwork process.
4. Recording objective anecdotal observations is the starting-point for daily team planning and the assessment process and is the evidence of the learning taking place in the setting.
5. Daily team planning is based on the parts of the daily routine; greeting time, plan-do-review, small group time and large group time.
6. HighScope teams plan by incorporating children's interests, children's developmental abilities, curriculum content (KDIs), classroom materials and adult ideas.
7. HighScope's summative assessment tool, the Child Observation Record, was designed to be used in all developmentally appropriate early childhood settings.
8. A summary of anecdotal observations in each curriculum-content area of the COR is used to form the basis of a family report to share at parent conferences.
9. To maintain and develop practice, HighScope has two observation-based curriculum assessment tools: the Programme Implementation Profile (UK) and Observation/Feedback.
10. The focus of curriculum assessment is on growth and development. Together the assessor and teachers recognise strengths and generate ideas for development.

Reflections on the HighScope approach

1. Working together
   - What were the characteristics of a team experience that you have enjoyed?
   - What are the advantages of team work?

- What are some of the problems with or barriers to teamwork?
- How are tasks divided in your classroom?

2. Child observations
   - How do you find out what children know?
   - How can you improve your observation skills so you all see things in a similar manner?
   - What do you use your observations for?

3. Decisions for children
   - How do you decide what to do in your classroom?
   - Do you know what your colleagues will be doing?
   - Where do you get your ideas from?

4. Child assessment
   - How do you assess children's learning and development?
   - What categories of development do you use?
   - Do you think it is right to score children's development?

5. Curriculum assessment
   - What methods do you use to maintain and develop your practice?
   - What are your classroom strengths?
   - What are your classroom areas for development?

References

Dewey, J. (1933) *How We Think: A Restatement of the Relation of Reflective Thinking to the Educative Process*. Boston: Heath

HighScope Educational Research Foundation (2002) *Infant Toddler Observation Record*. Ypsilanti, MI: HighScope Press

HighScope Educational Research Foundation (2003a) *Preschool Child Observation Record*. Ypsilanti, MI: HighScope Press

HighScope Educational Research Foundation (2003b) *Preschool Programme Quality Assessment* (PQA) (2nd edn). Ypsilanti, MI: HighScope Press

Likert, R. (1967) *The Human Organisation: Its Management and Value*. New York: McGraw-Hill

Lippitt, G. (1980) Effective Team Building Develops Individuality, *Human Resource Development* 4(1): pp. 13–16

Satir, V. (1988) *The New People Making*. Mountain View, CA: Science and Behaviour Books

Related reading

Boisvert, C. and Gainsley, S. (2008) *50 Activities for Large Groups*. Ypsilanti, MI: HighScope Press

Epstein, A. (2007) *Essentials of Active Learning in Preschool – Getting to Know the HighScope Curriculum*. Ypsilanti, MI: HighScope Press

Epstein, A. (2010) *Story Starters for Group Times*. Ypsilanti, MI: HighScope Press

Graves, M. (1996) *Planning Around Children's Interests*. Ypsilanti, MI: HighScope Press

Graves, M. (1997) *100 Small Group Experiences*. Ypsilanti, MI: HighScope Press

Graves, M. (2000) *The Essential Parent Workshop Resource*. Ypsilanti, MI: HighScope Press

Graves, M. (2007) *80 Activities for Small Groups*. Ypsilanti, MI: HighScope Press

HighScope Early Childhood Staff (2009) *Small Group Times to Scaffold Early Learning*. Ypsilanti, MI: HighScope Press

Hohmann, M., Weikart, D. P. & Epstein, A. (2008) *Educating Young Children. The Complete Guide to the HighScope Preschool Curriculum* (3rd edn). Ypsilanti, MI: HighScope Press

Marshall, B. (2007) *Lesson Plans for the First 30 Days*. Ypsilanti, MI: HighScope Press

8 The future

This chapter looks at the mission statement, current work and what lies ahead for the HighScope Educational Research Foundation in Michigan, USA and the international HighScope Institutes. It looks at the congruence of the HighScope approach with early years principles in the UK. Finally it summarises five key messages from HighScope which may help to guide our future thinking about early childhood.

Mission statement and work of the HighScope Educational Research Foundation

HighScope's mission is to lift lives through education. We envision a world in which students are partners with teachers in shaping the learning experience and become thoughtful, active and productive members of society. HighScope values knowledge, initiative, planning and reflection, encouragement, integrity and respect for all individuals and groups.

To carry out its mission HighScope's work comes under four strands:
- The development of curriculum and assessment products
- Professional development
- Early childhood evaluative research
- Advocacy of highly effective early childhood development programmes.

The constituents for these activities include teachers, caregivers, parents, administrators, researchers and policy makers and those who seek to influence them.

HighScope stands for highly effective early childhood development programmes and always has. The HighScope Perry Preschool Study led the way in convincing the world of the very possibility that high-quality early childhood education improves lives and that it is a good public investment with a strong economic return to taxpayers. Programme staff developed the HighScope Preschool Curriculum originally for their preschool programme. Thereafter HighScope resources and training have contributed to the professional development of early childhood educators around the world. HighScope advocacy focuses on encouraging public policies that support such programmes.

(HighScope Strategic Plan for 2011)

Strategic plans for the future are to continue to strengthen HighScope's position as an early childhood leader whose curriculum and assessment products, professional development offerings, research activities and advocacy contribute to highly effective early childhood development programmes. They will build on HighScope's reputation for high-quality work to deliver the message that the resources offered are up to date and applicable to all policies, practices and settings that support an interactive child development curriculum (HighScope Strategic Plan for 2011).

International institutes

The HighScope approach was designed to be disseminated and implemented, through publications and cascade training, across the full range of educational provision both in terms of age, sector and ability and across countries, cultures and economic backgrounds. Because daily planning revolves around children's interests and experiences, and materials are chosen to reflect children's homes and communities, the curriculum is adaptable in a wide variety of settings – across countries, cultures, languages, and socioeconomic groups. Its transferability and relevance have been clearly demonstrated in the development of international institutes in the following countries: Canada, Chile, Great Britain, Indonesia, Ireland, Mexico, the Netherlands, Portugal, South Africa and South Korea. For contact details see the 'International Institutes' under the About Us page of the HighScope website (www.highscope.org). In addition to the official institutes, HighScope training and practice is carried out in many other countries, including within the Caribbean and South America, Italy, Sweden and Turkey. The five-day Annual International Conference held in Michigan, USA draws together a worldwide gathering of hundreds of early childhood educators, researchers and policy makers. In addition, many of the international institutes also hold their own regular national or regional conferences.

HighScope and early years principles in the UK

Through a network of endorsed HighScope trainers in the UK over 3,000 practitioners have been trained on the eighteen-module HighScope Implementation Course to use the approach in their settings. It is estimated that 250,000 children have experience of the approach each year (www.high-scope.org.uk). These settings demonstrate how the principles underlying the HighScope approach are congruent with early years structures in the UK. The principles underlying the Early Years Foundation Stage introduced in England in September 2008 have much in common with the principles of the HighScope approach. The Early Years Curricula of Scotland (2007) and Northern Ireland (2006) and the Foundation Phase in Wales (2008) resonate with the core values found in HighScope.

The approaches set out in all the UK curriculum guidance documents reinforce the importance of active learning through first-hand experiences which build on what children already know. They advocate listening to children, observing closely to determine individual children's interests and ideas and using observational assessment to scaffold future learning. Adults are encouraged to view themselves as facilitators of children's self-initiated learning, promoting choice and independence, negotiation and collaboration, problem solving and risk taking.

Key messages from the HighScope approach

There are many stakeholders in developing and maintaining quality in highly effective early childhood programmes: politicians, parents, practitioners, managers, head teachers, advisers and administrators, often with different objectives. Among these diverse stakeholders there is nevertheless universal agreement about the adult traits necessary for success in any field, be it as a scientist, business executive, chef or plumber:

- initiative
- problem-solving ability

- planning ability
- capacity to work with and to have respect for others
- extended language use
- attaining standard academic goals in reading, maths, writing, science and so forth.

HighScope believes that in high-quality education all these values and traits must be engaged concurrently, and as appropriate to age-level capacity. It has identified the following five guiding principles of a high-quality programme that can be applied at all age levels, always remembering that adaptations will be necessary to allow for the physical and cognitive developmental level of the children involved.

- Education is most effective when learners plan activities, carry them out and reflect on their experiences with the support of adults and peers.
- The learner develops awareness and understanding through active involvement with people, materials, events and ideas.
- A variety of developmentally related active learning experiences contributes to the individual's intellectual, social, emotional and physical development.
- Consistent support and respect for personal decision making strengthens the individual's personal effectiveness and social responsibility.
- Scientific research produces knowledge, which contributes to the development of effective educational and social policies and programmes.

In its most general form, high-quality education is defined by the extent to which children are actively engaged in a rich learning environment with genuine opportunities for self-determined work and for in-depth conversations with adults and peers (Weikart, 2004 pp. 262–65).

I hope these key messages from HighScope, along with the 'Reflections on the HighScope approach' at the end of each chapter, will provide starting-points for reflection and discussion. Out of this may come a new understanding of what is important in early childhood and thoughtful ideas to apply this in practice.

The final words of this book come, appropriately, from Dr David P. Weikart, from whom we have learnt so much.

In the HighScope approach to early childhood education, adults and children share control. We recognise that the power to learn resides in the child, hence the focus on active learning practices. When we accept that learning comes from within, we achieve a critical balance in educating young children. The adults' role is to support and guide young children through their active learning adventures and experiences. I believe this is what makes our programme work so well.

(Hohmann, Weikart and Epstein 2008 p. 3)

References

A Curriculum for Excellence – Building the Curriculum 2: Active Learning in the Early Years (2007) Learning and Teaching, Scotland. http://www.ltscotland.org.uk/buildingyour curriculum/policycontext/btc/btc2.asp

Early Years Foundation Stage: Setting the Standards for Learning, Development and Care for Children from Birth to Five (2008). Department for Children, Schools and Families. http://nationalstrategies.standards.dcsf.gov.uk/node/157774

Framework for Children's Learning for 3 to 7 year olds in Wales (2008) assembly-publications @wales.gsi.gov.uk

Hohmann, M., Weikart, D. P. & Epstein, A. (2008) *Educating Young Children. The Complete Guide to the HighScope Preschool Curriculum* (3rd edn). Ypsilanti, MI: HighScope Press

Understanding the Foundation Stage (2006) Council for the Curriculum, Examinations and Assessment. www.nicurriculum.org.uk/foundationstage/index.aspBelfast www.ni curriculum.org.uk/docs/foundation_stage/UF_web.pdf

Weikart, D. P. (2004) *How HighScope Grew: A Memoir*. Ypsilanti, MI: HighScope Press

Websites

www.highscope.org (USA)
www.high-scope.org.uk (UK)
www.early-years.org (Ireland)

Index